Anything You Can Cook, I Can Cook Vegan

For Peter, my best friend

Richard Makin

Anything You Can Cook, I Can Cook Vegan

"You deserve buttery, New England-style lobster rolls, chorizo baked gnocchi, and a wedge of tres leches cake.... All this, everything I just mentioned, you can make vegan."

Welcome to the Plant Cult

Well, you finally did it; you joined a vegan cult. Now, take my hand as I crown you with a tiara made from miniature decorative gourds and tofu jerky: "One of us! One of us!" I'M JUST KIDDING. This isn't a cult! It's a cookbook, remember? You finally took the advice from that achingly cool friend Elsbeth (with a "B") and bought yourself a copy of *Anything You Can Cook, I Can Cook Vegan*. And you know what? I hate to hand it to Elsbeth-with-a-"B" like this, but she's right this time, you *really do deserve* this book. I take back everything I ever said about her.

You deserve this book because everyone deserves to know how to cook plants properly, whether you're a kitchen newbie or a veteran vegan chef. You know how drunk people at parties love to say we only use ten percent of our brain's potential? Well I think we only use ten percent of our veg crisper's potential. Sure, that bolognese you learned to cook from a YouTube tutorial tastes okay, but I'm here to tell you that you deserve better than okay! You deserve buttery, New England-style lobster rolls, chorizo baked gnocchi, and a wedge of tres leches cake. You deserve the glossiest French onion soup and a cheek-slapping slurp-fest with a bowl of shiitake ramen. You deserve to bourguignon the house down, then follow with a pan of glossy sea salt brownies and dalgona latte ice cream. I'm here to tell you that all this, everything I just mentioned, you can make vegan.

Daunted? Don't be, just stick with me. You see, I believe many of us are searching for a way to bust out of a kitchen rut, to break free from those four "it'll do" dishes we cook on rotation. We all love the idea of being adventurous in the kitchen, but the security of that safe, predictable YouTube bolognese can keep us from opening up our horizons. Like when you try to open the utensil drawer, but the potato masher inside has other plans. Your bolognese is that metaphorical potato masher, friend, and it's keeping you from opening up the drawer of life. *Holds your hand with both my hands, like a supportive aunt at your graduation.*

What if plant-based cooking were your escape route? What if you could satisfy your sense of adventure and *still* enjoy all your favorite meals? What if Nana's lasagne recipe that you've cooked every Saturday for the last sixteen years could somehow become exciting again? What if you stopped saying "what if"? Because the answer is obvs yes and you already bought a lovely big fat book about it.

And, hey, as the owner of this lovely big fat book, chances are you already know a bit about vegan food. You're probably already concerned about the ethical issues around eating animal products. You've most likely watched seventeen Netflix documentaries about plant-based eating and the climate crisis. But that's not necessarily why you finally listened to Elsbeth-with-a-"B" and bought this book.

You bought this book because it looks fun! I mean, come on… learning to make fish and chips out of eggplant? Yes, please! Whipping up a brisket sandwich from mushrooms? Sign me up! This book even has a snappy title, which is, weirdly, somehow uplifting and passive-aggressive at the same time. You see, I feel pretty strongly that the challenge of veganizing all your old favorite meals (and some of your future faves, too) is exactly what you need right now. *That's* the kind of excitement and carefully considered risk that could break you right out of that kitchen rut. With this book as your companion, and a little spring in your step, you'll pick up everything you need to become a plant-based kitchen boss and, OMG, it's going to be a majestic journey to watch! *Plunges fist into utensil drawer, rips out potato masher, and snaps it across knee triumphantly.*

Hi, I'm Richard

So, who am I to waltz in here like Hagrid, informing you of your magical plant-based destiny? Well, first of all, Hagrid doesn't waltz, he sashays, and second, I'm Richard, the School Night Vegan. My family calls me Chid, and you can, too, because I strongly suspect we already have one big thing in common: an interest in vegan food. Oh, boy, we're going to get on like a house, nay, *hotel* on fire!

I like to imagine that you've just rung my doorbell to introduce yourself (or perhaps to tell me that I've left my keys in the front door for the fourth time this week) and you can hear me thundering up from my basement kitchen with a dish towel over my shoulder and a pencil behind my ear. I fling open the door with a smile and you're greeted by the aroma of fresh bread and roasted garlic, a combo so pleasant that you *almost* ignore my staggeringly dirty apron and rather jarring socks and sandals. Understandably, your first question is, "Wow, what's cooking?" and, oddly, my answer is, "I don't know yet! But stick around and we'll find out."

You see, I'm not a chef, not by any formal (or informal) standard. I'm also definitely not a blogger, although that is how I tend to share my recipes. I'm more of an experimental vegan food scientist with too much time (and coffee) on his hands. This means I do things a little differently. When I cook, I set myself the challenge of taking apart a recipe, figuring out why it works, then piecing it back together… except using only plant-based ingredients. My dream is to take every dish I've ever loved and make it vegan.

Since I was a kid, I've been obsessed with food and cooking. My most vivid childhood memory is being picked up from school by Mam on a Friday, driving to our camper on a farm in Anglesey, Wales, and spending the weekend making chocolate bars from scratch. We made nougat, wafers, caramels, and fondant, layered them in whatever order we wanted, then dunked them in chocolate and waited impatiently for them to set. We even picked a name for our bars and designed their wrappers on sticky labels. Although I didn't know it then, that was my first weekend of recipe development.

Fast forward to 2015 and I had just started my first business selling hand-made ice-cream sandwiches out of a tiny blue van. If you think that sounds like a breeze, you're wrong. It was the hardest (and most expensive) thing I've ever done, but at least I learned how to hot-wire a vintage van with the engine of a moped. Weirdly, I also learned a lot about vegan food. I happened to share a professional kitchen with a gorgeous couple named Liz and Joe who ran Eat Chay, a vegan, Vietnamese street-food company.

They regularly fed me free lunches in exchange for uninvited Celine Dion lip-sync performances and murder podcast recommendations. I knew practically nothing about vegan food (despite being a long-time vegetarian) and, until that point, had always assumed that loving food and being vegan were incompatible. Being a vegan, I thought, involved sacrificing all your favorite foods in exchange for moral superiority and maybe a merit badge from Joaquin Phoenix. In reality, none of those things were true.

Joe and Liz guided me through my switch to veganism and I began experimenting with plant-based cooking. Instantly, I was hooked. I couldn't believe the joy that came with exploring a whole new world of food. I was using my obsessive love for recipe development and it felt magical! Still, making and selling ice cream took up every weekday and every weekend, so my opportunities for vegan kitchen experiments were strictly limited to school nights (aaaah, *now* that name makes sense). I'd clock off from churning thousands of liters of ice cream or baking hundreds of cookies, cycle home across London and start cooking all over again, but this time with plants. I'd think about a dish I couldn't live without and then work with an obsessive focus to create a vegan version that was indistinguishable from the original. *Cut to a flashback of me high-fiving myself over a vegan lasagne.*

I began to log my recipes on an Instagram account to make sure I didn't forget which ones had worked. I also put my food styling skills to good use and picked up a proper camera for the first time, to get some cracking shots. The Instagram algorithm gods must've been on my side, because things went a bit nuts, and before long I had lots of really cool, excited followers. Followers who also felt stoked about vegan cooking. Within a year I had closed my ice-cream business and sold my van, motivated by a new dream of making insanely good vegan food.

School Night Vegan is now my full-time job and I develop vegan recipes for magazines, newspapers, and restaurants. Sometimes, I still can't believe that it's my job to explore what the future of vegan cooking might look like. I never dreamed I'd get paid to nerd-out about plants. But my favorite part of what I do is helping other people nerd-out about plants, too.

And that's where this book comes in. Slap-bang in the middle of a pandemic, locked in my house with only my dog and a stack of *Buffy* DVDs for entertainment, I decided to write a cookbook. What better way to share my passion for vegan food and help other home cooks get the most out of their veggies? Nothing—except perhaps the musical episode of *Buffy*—could bring me more joy.

Introduction

So, Why Did I Write This Book?

These days, being vegan can mean all sorts of things. It can mean you're a diehard environmentalist or a teenage TikTok legend. It can mean you eat nothing but lentils or nothing but Lotus Biscoff spread (straight from the jar, obvs.). But, unfortunately, being vegan often still means missing out. In my six years as a vegan, plant-based offerings at restaurants and supermarkets have come a long way, but I think you and I can do even better. Making vegan food from scratch gives us the freedom to get creative with the kind of dishes we make. What's more, this book will show you how to cook each component part of a recipe, so you'll know exactly what's in your meal and you can dodge those store-bought vegan alternatives, if you choose.

Although I did set out to write a collection of vegan recipes, I hope you'll find this book is a lot more than that. Every recipe was developed, tested, styled, and photographed by me. No art director, no prop stylist, no photographer's assistant, just me and dog, Ripley, trying to trip me up every time I carried a plate of camera-ready food from one room to the next. Aside from revealing that I am a control freak, my hope is that in sharing a very exclusive, rather homemade slice of my *own* peculiar passion for vegan food, this book might help you uncover a unique culinary passion of your own.

To the newbie vegan chef, this book is a friendly, slightly overexuberant introduction to the world of vegan cooking. To the dedicated food lover, it's a manifesto on the versatility of vegan ingredients. And, for the experienced home cook, it's an open invitation to nerd-out with me over the magic of cooking with plants.

This book is my attempt to imagine a parallel universe where vegans can eat whatever they want, wherever they want. A full English breakfast at a greasy spoon! A bucket of crispy fried nuggets fresh from a fast food dive! A towering reuben sandwich at a bougie brasserie! Consider this book my attempt to write all that stuff into existence. Whether you're dining alone in a studio apartment or feeding a commune of thirty somewhere in the countryside, the recipes in this book will transport you to places you always assumed were vegan no-go zones.

It's also worth mentioning that I wrote this book because I'm a massive, unapologetic nerd. As I mentioned, School Night Vegan began as a way for me to keep track of my experiments with plants in the kitchen. Vegan food was a whole new subject for me back then, and I've been practicing some serious plant-based alchemy ever since. So, I guess, in a way, this book is also a collection of my lab notes. What kind of a vegan-mad scientist would I be if I kept all these rad ideas to myself? Sharing is caring, bestie!

Using This Book Like a Boss

If you're like me, you possess a chaotic-good energy that only allows you to read books out of sequence: not great for anything with a narrative, but probably fine for most cookbooks. However, if you're interested in cooking *this* book right, then start with this guide. These are my top tips to make sure you get the maximum amount of success out of my recipes, while having a blast at the same time.

Pick Your Recipe...

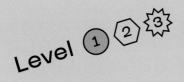

There are more than a hundred in this book, so take your time and find one you love. My recipes are separated by course or occasion and are all marked with a handy difficulty rating—the "level" at the bottom of a recipe page—so you can play it safe or get adventurous. And, if you need help deciding what to cook, use my Recipe Finder on page 22, which is like a quiz from a teen magazine, except it'll lead you to a delicious dinner instead of solving dating dilemmas.

... Then Read Your Recipe

Before you even enter the kitchen, ideally. Some of these dishes require unusual ingredients or specialized equipment and this is your chance to get ahead of the game. I want you to feel like that really camp 1960s version of Batman entering his bat cave when you walk into your kitchen: with a fully stocked utility belt and ready to kick butt! If you want to know why I'm calling for a particular ingredient, then look it up in The Plant-Powered Pantry (see pages 15–19) to learn what it's there for.

Make Any Subs

Every aspect of each recipe has been tested and tweaked to make sure it works. This is my gift to you: Merry Nerdmas. Where simple substitutions can be made, I've listed alternatives. By all means, play with my recipes—making swaps and changes is what creative cooking is all about—but once you go super-rogue, be prepared for different end results.

Make Any Building Block Recipes

Some of the dishes in this book are what I call Inception Recipes, because they feature one of my Building Block Recipes (see pages 226–273) within the main recipe. If you're confused by this reference because you haven't seen the movie *Inception*, don't worry, it's about Tom Hardy's lips, I think. That's all I can remember. Usually I'll provide a suggested quick substitution, in case you don't have much time, but if you do plan to go for it, be sure to make the Building Block Recipe first. I'll always include the page reference for any component that you need to make in advance.

Introduction

Take My Advice

Throughout the book I'll be answering real-life questions asked by real-life people about vegan cooking. I'm calling it Vegan Agony Aunt because that's sort of what it is, or at least a fun round of kitchen troubleshooting. Hopefully, these sections will help to answer some of your burning questions, too!

Have Fun!

I was tempted to label this step "FOLLOW MY INSTRUCTIONS TO THE LETTER," then I remembered I'm not Miss Trunchbull. Anxiety around cooking all comes from the fear of getting stuff wrong, so, remember: it doesn't matter! Greatness can only happen when we learn from our mistakes, and the most important part of cooking is having fun. Even if you have to order an emergency takeout for dinner because you blew up the stove trying to make seitan, at least you had a laugh doing it!

Measurements

I always recommend measuring your ingredients using electronic kitchen scales, unless we're talking about teaspoons and tablespoons. It's way more accurate and they're fairly cheap these days, but standard kitchen scales will work, too. Also, any ingredient measured in tablespoons or teaspoons should be level and not heaping.

Equipment

This book is for everyone: long-time legacy vegans and brand-new fresh-as-a-daisy vegans are both welcome here. However, I've become aware during the writing of this book that not everyone's kitchen is set up the same. As such, I've listed any specialized equipment before each recipe under "Equipment Needed" to give you a little heads-up. For instance, I use a high-speed blender throughout this book and I think you'll find it very useful if you have one, but don't worry, there are plenty of recipes you can make with equipment you already have in the kitchen.

A Note on Alcohol

Occasionally, in this book I'll use alcohol in a recipe. It's always there for a reason, but it's never essential, so if you're cooking for kids or for anyone who doesn't drink, feel free to omit it entirely.

... Oh, and one more thing. Some people get spooked when vegans use terms such as "chicken" or "cheese" to refer to plant-based products or recipes. Here's why I think it's important that those words appear in this book. When we sit down in a restaurant, our meal begins when we first pick up the menu. The words we read start to tell us a story of the food we're about to experience and they paint a picture of what to expect on our plate. The same applies here. If my recipe is designed to make you feel like you're eating a bucket of crispy fried chicken, I want you to know this from the second you turn the page. Calling it "Battered Wheat Protein Analog" tells you nothing about which flavors and textures to expect from my recipe. Plus, it sounds gross.

The Plant-Powered Pantry

As a friend, I feel like I can tell you this with love and compassion: your pantry needs an update. There, I said it. I wanted to tell you last week, but it was your birthday and your Nan told me not to spoil it for you. The fact is, decent vegan cooking isn't just about learning new techniques and following new recipes, it's about getting familiar with new ingredients. Some of these might sound rather alien, but that's part of the joy, isn't it? Shifting to a vegan diet involves relearning how to stock your pantry, so this is the first step in your brand-new kitchen plantasy.

Think, for a minute, about eggs. Over the last whatever-thousand years, people have figured out loads and loads of things to do with chicken eggs: cakes, scrambles, sauces, and soufflés among them. You might be tempted to say, "Wow, the humble egg; so versatile," but don't say that, not to me or my dog! Truth is, there's nothing magical about eggs, they've just been easy enough for people to steal from nests in relative abundance for a long time. Long enough for cooks to create lots and lots of eggy recipes.

For many of us, fifty percent of cooking is tradition and the other forty-nine percent is habit (the final one percent is listening to podcasts about serial killers). When you challenge yourself to remove an ingredient such as eggs from your kitchen, you rewrite those traditions and unpick those habits. And this is what I really love about vegan cooking: it forces us to be creative and adventurous in the kitchen while discovering new ingredients. I'm here to help you get to know them and what they do, so you can pack your cupboards and feel confident following the recipes in this book, or cooking off the cuff.

Vegan
Agony Aunt

What's the key to building a vegan pantry without taking out a bank loan?

It took me six years to figure out which ingredients I can't live without, and I'm still learning, so my advice is to take your time. I've made a list over the next few pages of some possibly unfamiliar ingredients that appear in this book more than once. It's a good place to start, but don't feel the need to splurge and buy everything all at once... that's how you end up with a 4lb (2kg) bag of something you don't know how to cook or pronounce. Definitely don't buy anything in bulk until you know that it will be a useful ingredient for you, and check out my list of suppliers (see page 275) if you need help finding anything.

1 Cannellini beans

Not just for chili sin carne! Blend an entire can (soaking water included) for a savory creamy sauce, ideal for stroganoff and pasta sauces (see pages 102 and 127).

2 Capers

Endlessly useful for adding piquant saltiness to any dish, but also for making vegan anchovy paste (see page 89). Reserve the caper brine, too, for making extra-fishy marinades.

3 Chickpeas

Always in unsalted water, please. That way, we can use the chickpeas for dinner and their soaking liquid (aquafaba) to make doughnuts for dessert.

4 Citrus

All lemons in this book are unwaxed, especially where you use the zest. But I always buy unwaxed anyway—even if I just need the juice—and zest them before juicing. The grated zest lasts for months in the freezer.

5 Cold-pressed rapeseed oil

Ideal for baking and frying with the added bonus of being egg-yolk yellow (which is also why you'll find it in my "If It Ain't Yolk" sauce, see page 269).

6 Gram flour

Made from ground chickpeas, this produces a convincingly eggy texture in batters, tofu scrambles, and vegan omelettes. It also keeps my vegan Parmesan cheese crumbly and craggy (see page 255).

7 Kala namak

Also known as "black salt" (but actually more pinkish in color) and found in traditional Indian cuisine. Its sulfurous taste lends an eggy flavor to sauces and tofu (see pages 34 and 269).

8 Kombu

Dehydrated kelp, found in many traditional Japanese recipes but also essential for making seafood alternatives (see page 79), thanks to its gently fishy but boisterously umami flavor.

9 Liquid smoke

Exactly what it says on the bottle and endlessly useful. Great for quick barbecue sauces and flavoring delicious vegan meats (see page 249).

10 Marmite

Love it or hate it, yeast extract is a true vegan flavor bomb. It adds meatiness to seitan recipes and transforms plant-based gravy (see pages 152 and 160). If you live outside Marmite's native UK and struggle to find that brand specifically, don't worry, any yeast or vegetable extract will do.

11 Massel stock

A completely vegan stock powder that you can buy in beef-, chicken- and pork-style flavors. It's one hundred percent natural, as well as gluten-free, and so useful for making meat substitutes and sauces (see pages 237, 240, 243, and 245).

12 Miso paste

Another traditional Japanese ingredient and vegan flavor bomb. Useful for replicating the savory flavor of meats and cheeses (see pages 235, 240, 255, and 256).

13 Nutritional yeast

Prized for its nutty, cheesy flavor with an umami kick. You'll find it in many vegan cheeses and cheesy sauces (see pages 70, 252, 255, 256, and 258).

The Plant-Powered Pantry

14 Plant milks

For the most part, I'll be using soy milk throughout this book. I recommend using a full-fat, unsweetened, and unflavored variety unless otherwise stated in the ingredients list of a recipe. Where other milks and yogurts are called for, the same applies: full-fat, unsweetened, and unflavored, please! If a recipe calls for coconut milk, I'm referring to the full-fat stuff in a can, not the watery stuff for drinking that comes in a carton.

15 Potato flour/starch

Great for keeping coatings crispy in the pan and a magical ingredient for making sliceable, grateable vegan cheeses (see pages 255 and 256).

16 Psyllium husk powder

A fiber powder made from seeds that behaves remarkably like eggs when hydrated. My go-to egg replacement in cakes and bakes (see page 199).

17 Rice flour/starch

Great for binding batters and pancakes, but also essential for convincingly textured fried and boiled eggs (see page 36).

18 Sunflower lecithin

Lecithin is what makes egg yolks great at thickening and emulsifying sauces, but a variety extracted from sunflower seeds is equally useful.

19 Tapioca flour

The secret ingredient behind stringy, stretchy vegan cheeses, such as my vegan mozzarella (see page 252).

20 Tempeh

Unlike tofu, tempeh is made from fermented whole soybeans, usually formed into a block. It's super tasty, high in protein, and can be sliced, cubed, or crumbled before cooking.

21 Tofu

Tofu comes in many different textures, and it's important to pay attention to which variety is called for in a recipe. I wouldn't recommend subbing silken tofu for firm tofu, or tofu skin for medium-firm. Stick to the variety stated in the ingredients list as much as possible.

21a Tofu—Extra firm

The firmest tofu, great for frying and grilling but also for shaving into thin, lacy slices for my vegan doner kebab (see page 77).

21b Tofu—Paper

Thin sheets of firm tofu with a particularly meaty texture. Makes wonderful vegan bacon and pepperoni once marinated (see pages 171 and 249).

21c Tofu—Silken

The softer side of tofu, with a slightly sweeter flavor and many applications, from cheesecakes to vegan boiled eggs.

21d Tofu—Yuba

Made from the skin that forms on heated soy milk, it adds a ribbony, eggy texture to tofu scrambles (see page 34).

22 TVP

Textured vegetable protein, soy chunks, ground soy... whatever you want to call it, it's an essential! Sold dehydrated in a variety of shapes (curls, chunks, ground, slices), it's an endlessly useful meat substitute that sucks up flavor like no other.

23 Vegan lactic acid

I use this stuff in vegan cheese-making (see pages 252–256). Lactic acid is what gives sharp mature dairy cheeses that tangy kick. A vegan version does exactly the same.

24 Vital wheat gluten

Isolated, powdered protein extracted from wheat and used for making the ancient Chinese meat substitute seitan (see pages 235–245).

Recipe Finder

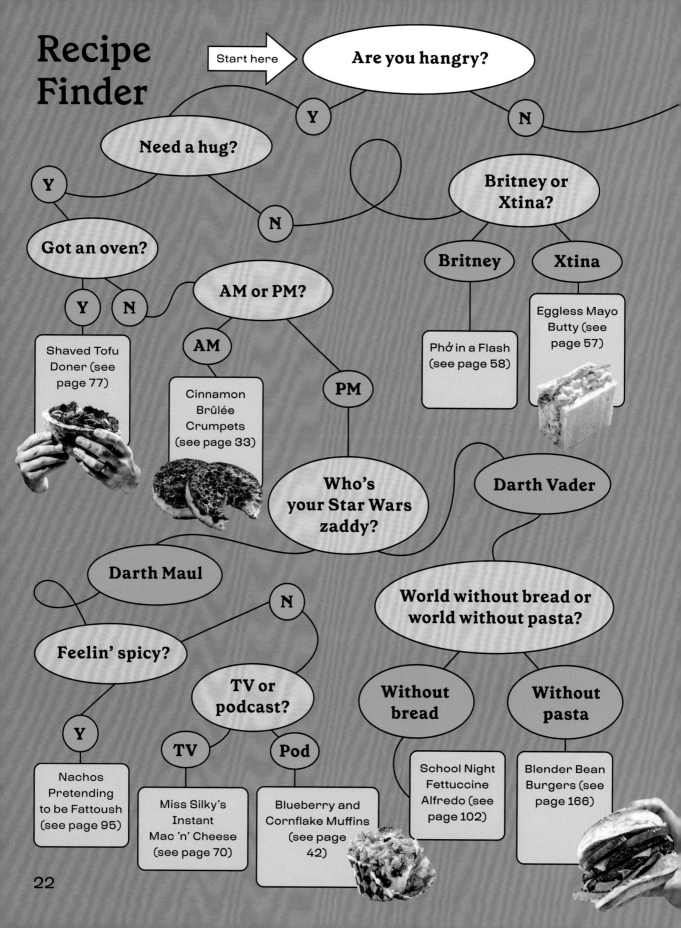

Start here → **Are you hangry?**

Y — **Need a hug?**

N — **Britney or Xtina?**

Need a hug?
- **Y** — **Got an oven?**
- **N** — **AM or PM?**

Britney or Xtina?
- **Britney** — Phở in a Flash (see page 58)
- **Xtina** — Eggless Mayo Butty (see page 57)

Got an oven?
- **Y** — Shaved Tofu Doner (see page 77)
- **N** —

AM or PM?
- **AM** — Cinnamon Brûlée Crumpets (see page 33)
- **PM** — **Who's your Star Wars zaddy?**

Who's your Star Wars zaddy?
- **Darth Vader** — **World without bread or world without pasta?**
- **Darth Maul** — **Feelin' spicy?**

Feelin' spicy?
- **Y** — Nachos Pretending to be Fattoush (see page 95)
- **N** — **TV or podcast?**

TV or podcast?
- **TV** — Miss Silky's Instant Mac 'n' Cheese (see page 70)
- **Pod** — Blueberry and Cornflake Muffins (see page 42)

World without bread or world without pasta?
- **Without bread** — School Night Fettuccine Alfredo (see page 102)
- **Without pasta** — Blender Bean Burgers (see page 166)

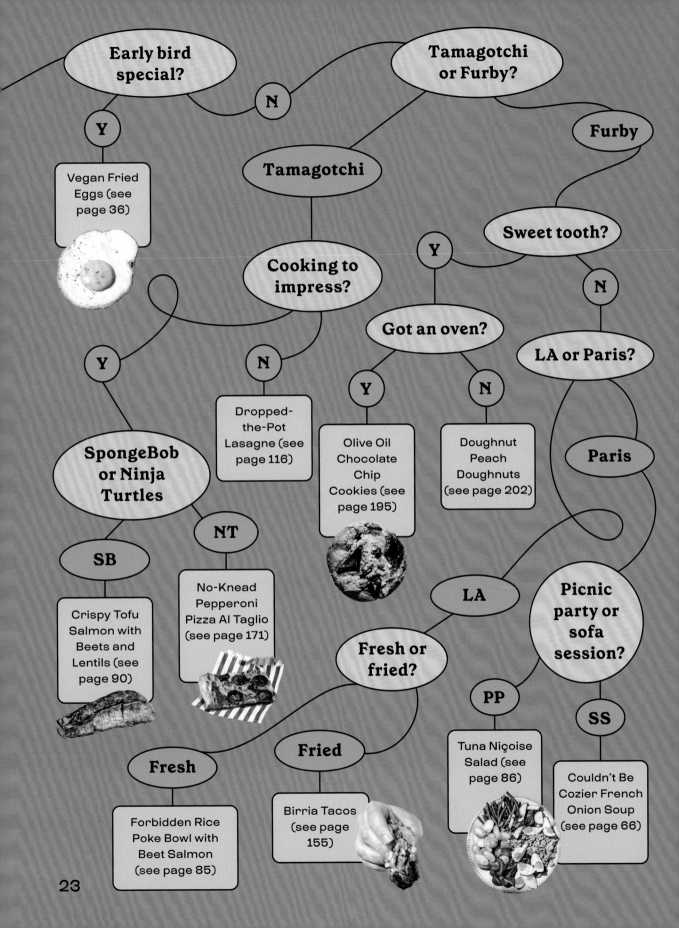

Early bird special?

Y — Vegan Fried Eggs (see page 36)

N

Tamagotchi or Furby?

Tamagotchi

Furby

Cooking to impress?

Sweet tooth?

Y — **Got an oven?**

N — **LA or Paris?**

Y

N

Cooking to impress?

Y — **SpongeBob or Ninja Turtles**

N — Dropped-the-Pot Lasagne (see page 116)

Got an oven?

Y — Olive Oil Chocolate Chip Cookies (see page 195)

N — Doughnut Peach Doughnuts (see page 202)

Paris

SpongeBob or Ninja Turtles

SB — Crispy Tofu Salmon with Beets and Lentils (see page 90)

NT — No-Knead Pepperoni Pizza Al Taglio (see page 171)

LA

Picnic party or sofa session?

Fresh or fried?

PP — Tuna Niçoise Salad (see page 86)

SS — Couldn't Be Cozier French Onion Soup (see page 66)

Fresh — Forbidden Rice Poke Bowl with Beet Salmon (see page 85)

Fried — Birria Tacos (see page 155)

Breakfast and Brunch

"My three favorite things all begin with Br-: Breakfast, Brunch, and Bruce Willis in that orange tank top from *Fifth Element*."

When she was eighteen, my highly influential, much cooler, older sister told me that her three favorite things in life began with "DC." I gripped my notepad tightly and took notes as she elaborated: Destiny's Child, Diet Coke, and *Dawson's Creek*.

Still dizzy from what I'd just heard, I wondered, "Will I ever be that cool?" The answer is no; I will die inferior. But, now that I'm older, I can at least say that, similarly, my three favorite things all begin with "Br-": Breakfast, Brunch, and Bruce Willis in that orange tank top from *Fifth Element*.

I mean it, breakfast and brunch are easily my favorite meals, but, boy, is it hard to find decent vegan food served before noon. Nothing beats a B&B breakfast or a cozy café brunch, but these places are so often vegan nightmare zones. My tip: do it yourself. This chapter has everything you need to make mind-blowing brekkies and next-level brunches from home—from plants!

Berry Custard Danishes

Makes 6

For the custard

1 cup (250ml) soy milk

½ teaspoon vanilla
bean paste

6 tablespoons (50g)
confectioners' sugar,
unsifted

¼ cup (30g) cornstarch

Pinch ground turmeric

1½ tablespoons
Vegan Butter

For the pastries

12oz (320g) pack ready-
rolled vegan puff pastry,
at room temperature

¼ cup (60ml) any plant milk

1 teaspoon vegetable oil

½ teaspoon agave syrup or
maple syrup

2oz (50g), about ⅓ cup
mixed berries, fresh
or frozen (or 6 canned
apricot halves)

2 tablespoons demerara
sugar

People often ask me why I've never written a croissant recipe, and the simple answer is that I don't actually like them very much (*zut alors*! I know...). It's a hot take, but I'd much rather have a Danish, packed with custard and fruit; it seems like so much more bang for your buck. Husband and I visited Copenhagen a few summers back, and I'll never forget the pastries from Landbageriet, a tiny vegan bakery there. This is my attempt at an easy, uncomplicated vegan Danish that you can customize with your favorite fruits.

To make the custard, place all the ingredients except the vegan butter in a medium saucepan and place over medium-low heat.

Whisk constantly until the mixture thickens dramatically, around 5 minutes. Once thickened, leave the mixture to bubble a couple of times before removing from the heat and vigorously whisking in the vegan butter.

Pour the custard into a baking pan (this will allow it to cool more quickly) and cover with parchment paper, making sure that the parchment is actually in contact with the surface of the custard. Once cooled to room temperature, refrigerate for a minimum of 20 minutes.

Remove the custard filling from the fridge and transfer to a bowl. Whisk vigorously until smooth. Set aside.

For the pastries, preheat the oven to 400°F (200°C) convection. Line a baking sheet with parchment paper.

Carefully unroll the pastry on to the prepared baking sheet and divide into 6 equal squares using a pizza cutter or sharp knife.

In a cup, mix together the plant milk, oil, and syrup. This will be your "egg wash." Using a pastry brush, apply a small amount of egg wash to the center of each square. Fold the corners of each square into the center and push them down gently to stick.

Put 1 heaping tablespoon of custard in the center of each pastry square. Follow with 1 tablespoon of mixed berries (or a canned apricot half, if using) and push gently into the custard.

Brush the exposed pastry with the remaining egg wash and sprinkle each pastry with 1 teaspoon demerara. Bake for 15–20 minutes, or until the pastries are golden brown.

Cinnamon Brûlée English Muffins

Makes 4

3½ tablespoons (50g)
    Vegan Butter (see page
    272), or store-bought
    vegan butter, at room
    temperature
¼ cup (35 g) light brown sugar
1 teaspoon ground cinnamon
4 English muffins

Is it a breakfast treat or is it the sneaky impulse snack of an astoundingly creative latchkey kid? The answer is both! I used to make these religiously in the lawless window between getting off the school bus and Mam's return home from work, so, naturally, I had to re-create them the instant I had a decent vegan-butter recipe. They taste even better than I remember and still work as currency for bribing your older brother into letting you watch four episodes of *Goosebumps* back to back.

In a small bowl, mash together the vegan butter, light brown sugar, and cinnamon with a fork until you have a smooth paste. Divide the paste between the tops of the 4 English muffins.

Place a large frying pan over low heat and leave for a few minutes to get hot. Place 2 of the crumpets bottom-side down in the pan and toast for around 30 seconds. Flip over on to their tops: you'll hear that the cinnamon butter will begin sizzling immediately. Leave to fry for 1 minute, making sure the caramel isn't burning.

Flip back over and swirl the English muffins around so their bottoms pick up any of the leaked butter and caramel. Toast for 30 seconds more before removing from the pan.

Leave to cool for a minute before serving, to allow the caramel to set on the top and bottom sides, while you continue to cook the remaining 2 English muffins in the same way.

Yuba Soft Scramble

☺ x 2

2oz (60g) yuba (see recipe note, below right)

7oz (200g) silken tofu

¼ cup (60ml) water

⅓ cup (45g) rice flour/starch

2 tablespoons cold-pressed rapeseed oil

Pinch ground turmeric

½ teaspoon kala namak (black salt), plus a pinch more to serve

1 tablespoon Vegan Butter (see page 272), or store-bought vegan butter

½ teaspoon finely chopped chives

Freshly ground black pepper

Equipment needed

High-speed blender (optional)

I like to imagine that, in another life, I'm a single, retired lady named Deborah who runs a vegan B&B in Florida. I tell all my guests that breakfast starts at seven, but I'll wake you up at five by banging pans around in the kitchen and singing Dolly Parton at the top of my lungs. All is forgiven, though, when you taste my vegan scrambled eggs. They're far from your standard tofu scramble, which people tend to pad out with veggies that don't belong there. Mine is silky-smooth and falls in ribbons and folds like Nanna's scrambles used to. At Deborah's, you come for the hospitality and stay for the scramble!

Place the yuba in a roasting pan and cover with just-boiled water. Leave to rehydrate for 5 minutes.

In the bowl of a high-speed blender, combine the silken tofu, water, rice flour, rapeseed oil, turmeric, and the ½ teaspoon kala namak. Blend until very smooth. Alternatively, place the ingredients in a tall container or bowl and blend with an immersion blender until very smooth.

Drain the rehydrated yuba, place in a bowl, and stir in the blended tofu mixture. The yuba will naturally tear apart into smaller pieces. Don't worry.

Heat a frying pan over medium heat and add the vegan butter. Once the pan is hot, pour in the yuba mixture. Cook without stirring for about 30 seconds, then gently stir with a spatula. Continue like this until the mixture is no longer wet-looking and the texture resembles lightly cooked eggs.

Remove from the pan and sprinkle with a pinch each of kala namak, black pepper, and chives before serving, on toast, if you like.

> **Recipe note**
> For the body of the scramble, this recipe uses yuba, which is a type of tofu made and dried in thin, flat sheets. You'll need to rehydrate it for a few minutes before use to get that ribbony soft-scramble texture. If you can't get hold of yuba, this recipe will still be delicious with crumbled firm tofu, but the texture won't be quite as convincing.

Vegan Fried Eggs

Makes 6

7oz (200g) soft silken tofu
(see recipe note,
below right)
6 tablespoons rice flour
1½ tablespoons vegetable oil
¼ teaspoon kala namak
(black salt)
2 tablespoons Vegan Butter
(see page 272), or store-
bought vegan butter
¾ cup (175ml) "If It Ain't Yolk"
Sauce (see page 269)
Freshly ground black pepper

Equipment needed
High-speed blender (optional)

Vegan Agony Aunt

<u>What is black salt and how
do I use it?</u>
Black salt is another name
for kala namak, which is a
type of Himalayan rock salt
with a characteristically eggy
flavor and smell. It's been
used for a very long time in
Indian cooking in dishes,
such as pani puri, and cool
summer drinks, such as
nimbu pani. In this recipe,
it helps to make our fried
eggs taste really authentic.
It appears a few times
throughout this book, so if
you're after a convincingly
eggy experience, or you're
building a bulletproof
vegan pantry, this is a hero
ingredient for you!

**A staple of greasy-spoon caffs everywhere: the humble fried egg!
My vegan version is so quick and easy to make that you'll be shooketh
to the core. My pro tip is to fry them in vegan butter so they get a gorgeous
ring of crispy lace around the edges, just like a real egg, with a jiggly but
firm center. Top with a little of my "If It Ain't Yolk" Sauce and you'll be one
step closer to the vegan full English breakfast of your dreams.**

Place the silken tofu, rice flour,
vegetable oil, and kala namak in
the bowl of a high-speed blender.
Blend until completely smooth.
(If you're using firm silken tofu,
you may need to add 1 tablespoon
water to make the mixture blend
smoothly.) Alternatively, place
the ingredients in a tall container
and blend with an immersion
blender until very smooth.

Place a medium-sized frying
pan for which you have a lid over
medium heat and cover with the
lid. Heat for around 2 minutes.
Add one-third of the vegan butter
to the pan and swirl to coat the
bottom. Reduce the heat to low.

Using an ice cream scoop or
serving spoon, carefully spoon
2 fried egg–sized portions of
the white mixture (around
3 tablespoons each) into the pan,
making sure the 2 eggs don't
touch. Immediately cover with
the lid and leave to cook for
3–5 minutes.

Remove the lid and flip the
eggs if you like them over easy.
Otherwise, remove from the pan.
Serve with 2 tablespoons of "If It
Ain't Yolk" Sauce per egg and a

little black pepper, on toast, if
you like.

Repeat to fry another 4 eggs,
again, 2 at a time.

Recipe note
Silken tofu comes in all sorts of
textures, ranging from extra-
firm to extra-soft. All silken tofu
works for this recipe, but if you
use firm or extra-firm you may
need to loosen things up with
an extra 1–2 tablespoon water.
Don't add too much though,
or your eggs will be thin and
may not cook to a firm texture.
You're also using black salt for
egginess. The more you add,
the more authentic your eggs
will taste, but, remember, it's
salt, so use it sparingly.

Whipped Almond Ricotta Toast with Basil Oil

Makes 2

For the whipped ricotta

2 quantities Almond Ricotta (see page 258)
2 tablespoons extra-virgin olive oil
2 teaspoons lemon juice
Sea salt flakes

For the basil oil

1oz (30g) bunch basil, plus basil leaflets, to serve
½ cup (120ml) extra-virgin olive oil, or cold-pressed rapeseed oil

For the toast

1 tablespoon Vegan Butter (see page 272), or store-bought vegan butter
2 thick slices sourdough bread
Freshly ground black pepper

"Hang on, are we reading a cookbook or scrolling through TikTok? Wow: what a trendy recipe! This Richard Makin guy must be really cool and in touch with the fleeting desires of Gen Z, despite being very, very old!" is what you're undoubtedly thinking right now. And you'd be right! As an honorary member of Gen Z, I couldn't write this book without featuring my vegan take on at least one TikTok recipe. *Puts on bifocals and reads from a sheet of paper*: "It's the almond ricotta for me… not in the least bit sus… I like to eat mine while listening to my Belly Eyelash records, fellow kids."

To make the whipped ricotta, place the almond ricotta in the bowl of a stand mixer fitted with the whisk attachment, then add both the olive oil and lemon juice with 1 teaspoon sea salt flakes. Whip until light and fluffy, around 2 minutes. Alternatively, whip the ricotta with a hand whisk in a bowl. Transfer the almond ricotta to a piping bag and cut a ⅝in (1.5cm) hole from the tip. Set aside.

For the basil oil, place the basil (stems and all) in a blender or food processor with the oil. Pulse-blend until coarsely blended. If you have time, transfer the blended olive oil to a jar, seal with a lid, and leave to infuse overnight. If you're in a hurry, skip to the next step.

Pass the infused oil through a fine nut-milk bag, or rest a sheet of muslin in a sieve over a bowl and pour the oil through. Discard the basil pulp and set the oil aside.

To make the ricotta toast, place a medium-sized frying pan over medium heat. Butter both sides of the sourdough bread and place in the frying pan to toast. Flip once browned, around 1 minute. Remove from the pan and allow the toast to cool for a minute.

Pipe the almond ricotta on to the toasts, drizzle with some of the basil oil, scatter with tiny basil leaves, and top with ¼ teaspoon pepper and a pinch more sea salt flakes before serving.

The leftover basil oil will keep in an airtight container in the fridge for up to 2 weeks.

Bodega Bagels

Makes 2

2 large New York-style
  bagels, halved
2 tablespoons Vegan Butter
  (see page 272), or store-
  bought vegan butter
1lb (450g) block extra-firm
  tofu, drained
4 teaspoons vegetable oil
Pinch kala namak (black salt)
4 slices vegan American
  cheese
1 quantity Paper Tofu Bacon
  (optional, see page 249),
  freshly prepared and hot
Freshly ground black pepper

A few years ago, Husband and I spent Thanksgiving in New York. The only issue was that we didn't actually realize it was Thanksgiving, so when all the restaurants were closed on a random Thursday, we panicked. We had to ask a Brooklyn bodega clerk in our most English accents what was happening before we realized our mistake. She must've heard our tummies rumbling, because she offered us some fresh bagels instead. I had mine with grilled tofu and glossy vegan American cheese: a bagel I'll never forget! This recipe is my homage to that life-saving bagel, with added vegan bacon for good measure.

Preheat the broiler and place a baking sheet at the bottom of the oven.

Place the halved bagels on a separate baking sheet, cut sides up, and toast until lightly browned. Remove from under the broiler and transfer to a cutting board. Spread with the vegan butter and set aside.

Slice the extra-firm tofu into 4 large rectangles, rub both sides with 2 teaspoons vegetable oil, and arrange on the baking sheet. Sprinkle with the kala namak and a pinch of pepper. Place under the broiler for around 5 minutes, or until lightly browned, before flipping and repeating with the other side.

Once the second side is browned, top each piece of tofu with a slice of vegan American cheese and return under the broiler until the cheese is just melted.

Fill the toasted bagels with the cheese-topped grilled tofu and the bacon, then sandwich together, wrap in parchment paper, and serve.

Blueberry and Cornflake Muffins

Makes 12

For the cornflake topping
2 tablespoons Vegan Butter (see page 272), or store-bought vegan butter, chilled

2 tablespoons demerara sugar

1 cup (30g) cornflakes

For the muffins
½ cup (120ml) soy milk, at room temperature

2 teaspoons lemon juice

¼ cup (60 ml) water

¼ cup (60 ml) vegetable oil

1½ teaspoons psyllium husk powder (or 3 teaspoon ground flaxseed)

2½ cups (320g) all-purpose flour

2½ teaspoons baking powder

4 tablespoons (65g) Vegan Butter (see page 272), or store-bought vegan butter, at room temperature

1 cup (200g) granulated sugar

2 teaspoons vanilla extract

5oz (150g) blueberries

Fine sea salt

Here, I made you some breakfast that's actually cake in disguise. It's topped with cornflakes and packed with blueberries, so you can trick your colleagues into thinking it's a bowl of cereal, but secretly we'll know that you're about to have the best morning of your life.

To make the topping, place the vegan butter and demerara sugar in a bowl. Using your fingertips, rub them together until you have a lumpy, sandy mixture. Add the cornflakes and rub in gently with your fingers, being careful not to break the cornflakes too much. Set aside.

For the muffins, preheat the oven to 350°F (180°C) convection. Line a 12-hole muffin pan with paper liners. Set aside.

In the bowl of a blender, combine the soy milk, lemon juice, water, vegetable oil, and psyllium husk powder. Blend on high speed until smooth, then set aside.

In a bowl, combine the flour, baking powder, and ½ teaspoon salt. Whisk together and set aside.

In the bowl of a stand mixer fitted with the paddle attachment, or in a bowl with a handheld electric mixer, beat together the vegan butter, granulated sugar, and vanilla extract until light and fluffy, around 2 minutes.

Add half the soy milk mixture to the bowl of the stand mixer and beat to combine. Now add half the flour mixture and beat on low speed until just combined. Repeat the process with the second half of the soy milk mixture and the flour mixture.

Remove the bowl from the stand mixer and add the blueberries. Mix by hand carefully, using a spatula, until just distributed.

Divide the mixture among the 12 muffin liners. Divide the cornflake topping among the muffins, being careful not to let any fall off onto the pan. Place in the preheated oven and bake for 30–35 minutes. Watch the muffins closely for the last 5 minutes of baking to make sure the cornflakes don't burn.

Once baked, the muffins should be domed and the cornflake topping should be golden. Remove from the oven and place on a wire rack. Allow to cool fully before serving.

Classic Johnnycakes

☺ x 2–4

1¾ cups (450ml) any
   plant milk
1 tablespoon lemon juice
2 teaspoons vanilla extract
1¾ cups (200g) self-rising
   flour
⅞ cup (110g) cornmeal
   (coarse-ground polenta)
1 teaspoon baking powder
3 tablespoons sugar
1 tablespoon Vegan Butter
   (see page 272), or store-
   bought vegan butter,
   plus more to serve
Fine sea salt
Maple syrup, to serve

An easy family favorite, ideal for pretending you're in an American diner, face half-obscured by a tower of pancakes. Top tip: This recipe also makes perfect waffles in a waffle iron, or as I like to call them, carb-based linear grid cakes. Regardless of how you cook them, serve with maple syrup and vegan butter or face the consequences!

To make the "buttermilk," combine the plant milk, lemon juice, and vanilla extract. Whisk lightly and set aside. The mixture will look slightly curdled.

In a separate bowl, beat together the self-rising flour, cornmeal, baking powder, sugar, and a pinch of salt.

Add the buttermilk mixture to the dry ingredients and mix until just combined and no lumps remain.

Lightly butter a large frying pan or non-ridged griddle pan with the 1 tablespoon vegan butter. Place over medium-low heat and bring to temperature. If you don't plan to serve the pancakes straight from the pan, preheat your oven to around 175°F (80°C) convection and line a baking sheet with parchment paper.

Test a small amount of pancake batter in the center of the pan to check that it's the right temperature: within 30–40 seconds, bubbles should start to appear on the surface of the tester pancake. Once all the bubbles have popped, flip the pancake over using a silicone spatula. The underside should be golden brown.

Repeat to cook the rest of the batter, keeping the pancakes 3–5in (7.5–12.5cm) in size. If necessary, keep the cooked pancakes warm in the preheated oven. It's important not to overcrowd the frying pan, so be prepared to make these in batches.

Serve with maple syrup and a little vegan butter.

Leek & Marmite Cheesy Wheels

2 leeks

3 tablespoons Vegan Butter (see page 272), or store-bought vegan butter

¼ cup (60ml) white-wine vinegar

Pinch sugar

All-purpose flour, to dust

18oz (500g) package vegan puff pastry

4 tablespoons Marmite

3 tablespoons soy milk

3 tablespoons white sesame seeds

2oz (50g) vegan cheese, grated (make sure it's a melting variety)

Inspired by the cheesy swirls at Pophams Bakery in Hackney, London, these crispy fellas deliver a double dose of cheesy Marmite goodness straight to the face. They're in the brunch section because savory pastries in the morning feel sophisticated, but I regularly eat these for lunch with a can of beans, because I'm an adult who gets to decide stuff about my own life.

Remove the green tops of the leeks and slice in half lengthwise. Wash the leeks, making sure there's no grit trapped between the layers. Slice the leeks lengthwise again, into long quarters, then finally slice the quartered leeks in half widthwise, making sure they'll fit in your largest frying pan.

Heat a large frying pan for which you have a lid over medium-low heat. Add the vegan butter. Once melted, add the leeks to the pan in a snug row, cut sides facing down. Add the vinegar and sugar and bring to a simmer. Once the vinegar has evaporated by roughly half (5–8 minutes), use a pair of tongs to flip the leeks so the cut sides are facing up. Cook for another 5–8 minutes, or until the bottom sides are lightly browned.

Once all the vinegar has evaporated and the leeks are softened, they are done. If the leeks are still firm, add a few tablespoons of water, cover with the lid, and let cook for another 3–5 minutes, or until the water has evaporated and the leeks are soft.

Remove the leeks from the pan and peel off the browned outer leaves, leaving only the soft inner leaves. Coarsely chop into shreds and spread out on a small baking sheet to cool.

While the leeks cool, preheat the oven to 350°F (180°C) convection.

Lightly dust a work surface with flour and roll out the puff pastry to a 16 ½ x 11in (42 x 28cm) rectangle. Use a palette knife or bench scraper to spread the Marmite over the pastry. Spread the cooled, sliced leeks over the entire surface.

Starting with a short edge, roll the rectangle of pastry up to create a thick, 11in- (28cm-) long snake. Brush the roll all over with a little soy milk and sprinkle with the sesame seeds. Use a serrated knife to slice into 10 roughly 1 ¼in (3cm) rolls. Lay them, spaced well apart, on a lined baking sheet, or you may need 2 sheets. (At this point, you can freeze them until hard, then transfer to an airtight container and return to the freezer. They keep for 1 month.)

Gently brush the rolls again with a little more soy milk and top with the grated vegan cheese, dividing it equally between them. Bake in the oven for 35–40 minutes.

Remove from the oven and allow to cool fully before serving.

Brunch Burrito

Makes 1

For the filling

3 frozen hash browns
2 ripe tomatoes, quartered
2 teaspoons liquid smoke
Pinch smoked paprika
2 teaspoons soy sauce
1 ripe avocado
Leaves from a small bunch
   of cilantro
Juice ½ lime
Sea salt flakes

For the egg tortilla

¾oz (20g) yuba
2oz (65g) silken tofu
1½ tablespoons water
¼ cup (30g) rice flour
1 tablespoon cold-pressed
   rapeseed oil
Pinch ground turmeric
1 large flour tortilla
½ teaspoon kala namak
   (black salt)
3 slices vegan American
   cheese

Equipment needed

High-speed blender (optional)

An entire brunch in a burrito? You betcha—minus the bottomless mimosas! I'm particularly proud of the vegan egg in this little bundle of joy. It's similar to my yuba scramble, except it's fried like a flat omelet then topped with a flour tortilla. It makes the rolling process much easier and the eating less messy.

Preheat the oven to 400°F (200°C) convection and place the hash browns on a baking sheet.

Place the quartered tomatoes in a small bowl and toss with the liquid smoke, smoked paprika, soy sauce, and a pinch of sea salt flakes. Transfer to a small roasting pan.

When the oven is hot, put in the hash browns and tomatoes and bake for around 20 minutes, or until the hash browns are golden and the tomatoes are gently roasted.

Meanwhile, remove the pit from the avocado and scoop out the flesh. Coarsely chop, then place in a bowl. Add the cilantro and lime juice and gently stir to combine. Cover and set aside.

For the egg tortilla, place the yuba in a roasting pan and cover with just-boiled water. Leave to rehydrate for 5 minutes.

In a blender (ideally a high-speed blender), combine the silken tofu, water, rice flour, rapeseed oil, and turmeric. Blend until very smooth. Or blend the ingredients in a bowl with an immersion blender until very smooth.

Drain the hydrated yuba and place in a bowl. Stir in the blended tofu mixture. The yuba will naturally tear apart into smaller pieces. Don't worry.

Place a nonstick frying pan for which you have a lid over medium heat. Once hot, add the yuba mixture, then immediately top with the tortilla. Reduce the heat to low and cover the pan. Cook for 2 minutes, or until the underside is lightly browned, then flip and allow the tortilla to toast gently for 1 minute more.

While the tortilla toasts, sprinkle the "egg" side with the kala namak and place over the vegan cheese. Cover with a lid to help the cheese melt and cook for a final minute.

Remove the tortilla from the pan and place tortilla-side down on a sheet of foil. Top with the avocado, hash browns, and roasted tomatoes in a strip down the center.

Fold the left and right sides of the tortilla over the ends of the strip of filling by about ⅝in (1.5cm) to make sure it doesn't fall out the sides when rolled. Roll the burrito neatly. Wrap tightly in the foil and serve immediately.

Tof-Egg Shakshuka

☺ x 3

For the tof-eggs
8oz (200g) firm silken tofu
¼ cup (30g) rice flour/
  starch (see recipe note,
  below right)
1½ tablespoons vegetable oil
3 tablespoons water
1 teaspoon kala namak
  (black salt)

For the shakshuka
2 tablespoons olive oil
1 onion, coarsely chopped
3 garlic cloves, crushed or
  finely grated
1 teaspoon ground cumin
1 teaspoon smoked paprika
¼ teaspoon cayenne pepper
2 x 14oz (400g) cans whole
  tomatoes
16oz (460g) jar roasted red
  peppers, drained and
  coarsely chopped
2 tablespoons tomato purée
1 tablespoon sugar
Small bunch parsley, leaves
  coarsely chopped or torn
⅓ cup (80ml) "If It Ain't Yolk"
  Sauce (optional, see
  page 269)
Sea salt and freshly ground
  black pepper

Equipment needed
High-speed blender (ideally)

As a vegetarian, my go-to brunch dish was shakshuka, because it's bold, grown-up, and a great excuse to eat spicy food from the second you wake up. But as a vegan, brunch became a minefield: what is shakshuka without eggs? Can I just serve shakshuka sauce without eggs? The answer is no. I've tried, and I lost three friends over it. So I worked hard like a motivated lab technician to develop a way to poach tofu as though it were an egg, bubbling away in that spicy, rich sauce... and, hey, presto! Brunch is saved!

Place the tof-egg ingredients in a blender (ideally a high-speed blender) and blend until very smooth. Set aside. Alternatively, blend the ingredients in a tall container or bowl using an immersion blender until very smooth.

Preheat the oven to 400°F (200°C) convection.

Place a cast-iron, ovenproof frying pan for which you have a lid over medium-low heat and add the olive oil. Once hot, add the onion and garlic and fry for 1 minute. Add the spices and stir to combine.

Using a fork, remove the tomatoes from the can (leaving behind the sauce, which you can reserve and add later to pasta sauce, see page 270) and add to the pan. Crush the tomatoes gently with a fork, then add the red peppers, tomato purée, and sugar. Stir to combine and bring to a simmer. Once bubbling, cover and transfer to the hot oven for 20 minutes.

Remove from the oven, taste the sauce, and season with salt and pepper.

Make 6 wells in the shakshuka sauce and spoon around 3 tablespoons of the tof-egg mixture into each. Cover again with the lid and return to the oven for 10 minutes more.

Remove from the oven and remove the lid. The tof-eggs should have poached firm.

Sprinkle the shakshuka with the parsley and top each of the tof-eggs with "If It Ain't Yolk" Sauce, if using. Serve with crusty sourdough toast.

> **Recipe note**
> For the tof-egg, be sure to avoid glutinous rice flour, as it'll make everything gummy like mochi. Plain rice flour/starch is what you're after.

Lunch

"This chapter is packed with shortcuts to dream lunches that you'll be tempted to eat at 10:09 a.m."

Everybody's got that one colleague who takes joy from peering over your shoulder right as you crack open your lunch of embarrassing leftovers to say, "Ooh, what's he got today?" If you must know, Patricia, it's leftover takeout from three days ago and, yes, my lunch box is now permanently stained with turmeric and regret.

But, with more of us working from home than ever before, free from Patricia's judgmental gaze, making lunch has become another opportunity for unbridled creativity! This chapter is packed with shortcuts to dream lunches that you'll be tempted to eat at 10:09 a.m., such as my Phở in a Flash or Miss Silky's Instant Mac 'n' Cheese (see pages 58 and 70). You might be on the clock, but your lunch can still rock.... Please don't cancel me for that last remark.

And forget everything you know about vegan salads. Take every thought of unfortunate dry chickpeas and suspicious mushy leaves and banish them to the darkest corners of your mind. Done? Good, now we can continue. These vegan salads are joyous affairs packed with big bold flavors and unapologetic textures. They are the main event and simply couldn't be any further from your boomer uncle's notion of rabbit food.

You'll find some slightly more involved recipes here, too, for days when you can dedicate your full attention to lunch, such as my Seitan Reuben or Tuna Niçoise Salad made with delicious vegan boiled eggs (see pages 73 and 86). Whatever you choose to make, I hope this is the kind of lunch you can't stop thinking about until dinner.

Eggless Mayo Butty

Makes 4

9oz (250g) medium-firm tofu, or firm silken tofu

3½oz (100g) canned cooked ackee (see recipe note, below right)

¼ cup (60ml) Ten-Second Mayo (see page 262), or store-bought vegan mayo

1 teaspoon Dijon mustard

¼ teaspoon kala namak (black salt)

1 tablespoon finely chopped chives

Small bunch cress

8 slices white bread

4 large leaves cos, gem, or romaine lettuce

Sea salt and freshly ground black pepper

The humble egg mayo butty (as they're affectionately known in the UK) is the only sandwich suitable for both a quick bite and a fancy afternoon tea (crusts off, pinkies up!), so I just had to make a vegan option. My plant-based egg mayo is just as versatile, creamy, and protein-packed as the OG, plus it involves zero cooking, so it's super easy to make.

Drain the tofu and slice into ¼in (5mm) cubes. Carefully place on a sheet of paper towel and pat dry with a second sheet. Set aside.

Open the can of cooked ackee and drain it through a strainer. Run it under the faucet to wash off the brine, then set aside.

In a bowl, whisk together the vegan mayo, Dijon mustard, and kala namak. Add the cubed tofu and ackee. Stir very gently to combine, trying to break as few of the cubes of tofu and chunks of ackee as possible.

Finally, add the chives and cress, then season to taste, if necessary.

Divide the filling between 4 slices of the bread, top with lettuce, and follow with the remaining 4 slices of bread. Slice and serve.

> **Recipe note**
> This recipe uses precooked canned ackee to simulate cooked egg yolk. If you haven't heard of ackee, please don't assume it was invented in a lab by vegans in white coats. It's been used in cooking for a very long time and plays a huge part in traditional West African and Jamaican cuisine. Often served alongside salt fish, it's a fruit with buttery yellow flesh and a delicious but subtle savory flavor.

Phở in a Flash

☺ x 1

1 small carrot

3 slices tofu, or 1oz (25g) soy chunks

3½oz (100g) fine rice noodles (not egg noodles!)

1 teaspoon onion powder

1 cinnamon stick, snapped

1 star anise

¼ teaspoon Chinese 5 spice

½ teaspoon light brown sugar

2½ teaspoons vegan bouillon powder

1oz (25g) beansprouts

1 red chili, sliced

4 mint sprigs

4 cilantro sprigs

4 basil sprigs

½ lime, sliced

A few minutes of prep for a whole lot of pleasure! This is my *almost* instant take on the Vietnamese noodle soup, and it's a total slurp-fest: you just need to add boiling water. In seconds, you'll have a spiced broth with fresh aromatic herbs and veggies. Call your boss into the break room and tell them to watch you prepare it literally in minutes; if they don't immediately give you employee of the month for this innovation, it's time to walk. You're a lunch-break genius, and you deserve to be applauded!

Use a veggie peeler or julienne peeler to shave the carrot into either wide ribbons or thin strips. Put them into a large heatproof jar (if you can find one that is around 24oz [700ml] in volume, that would be perfect).

Heat a dry nonstick frying pan or cast-iron skillet over medium heat and add the slices of tofu, if using. Cook for 3–5 minutes on each side, or until lightly grilled. Remove from the pan and allow to cool, before adding to the jar.

Put the remaining ingredients into the jar, in layers, with the soy chunks, if using, and placing the chili, herbs, and lime slices on top, then seal tightly. Keep refrigerated until lunchtime.

To serve, remove the lid and take out the chili, herbs, and lime slices. Boil a kettle and pour 2½ cups (600ml) boiling water into the jar.

Cover loosely with the lid and leave for 5 minutes, then remove the lid and stir well. Put the lid back on and leave for another 2 minutes.

Transfer the phở to a bowl and top with the chili, herbs, and lime slices. Or return those to the jar and eat straight from that.

Miso Shallot Grilled Cheese

Makes 2

For the miso shallots

3 tablespoons white or red miso paste

5½ tablespoons (80g) Vegan Butter (see page 272), or store-bought vegan butter, melted

2 cups (450ml) just-boiled water

8 shallots, halved

Leaves from 3 thyme sprigs

Freshly ground black pepper

For the sandwiches

2 tablespoons Vegan Butter (see page 272), or store-bought vegan butter, at room temperature

4 thick slices white bloomer

2 tablespoons Ten-Second Mayo see page 262), or store-bought vegan mayo

1 quantity Vegan Mozzarella (see page 252), or vegan melting cheese

Sea salt flakes

I've been dreaming up ways to jazz up a grilled cheese for ages now… and I really think I've cracked it with this recipe. The shallots are braised slowly in a buttery miso broth that leaves them caramelized and gorgeously browned. They're then shredded and added to a vegan mozzarella-stuffed sandwich before it's grilled. The whole experience is an exercise in umami magic, and I challenge you not to call your mom to announce your life-changing experience after the first bite.

To make the miso shallots, preheat the oven to 400°F (200°C) convection.

In a bowl, whisk together the miso, vegan butter, water, and ½ teaspoon pepper until smooth. Add the halved shallots and thyme and stir to coat.

Transfer everything to a small roasting pan. Cover tightly with foil and place in the oven to bake for 30 minutes.

Remove the foil and stir well to combine. Return to the oven, still uncovered, for another 15 minutes, then allow to cool while you make the sandwiches.

For the sandwiches, spread the vegan butter over 1 side of each slice of bread. Spread the vegan mayo over the unbuttered sides.

Place 2 slices of bread on top of the mayo with the vegan mozzarella, spreading it right to the edges. Season to taste.

Put the shallots on a cutting board and coarsely slice. Distribute them over the mozzarella and close the sandwiches, buttered sides facing out.

Place a large frying pan over medium heat. When hot, place a sandwich in the center of the pan and press down with a heavy lid. Grill until golden brown underneath, then flip and repeat.

Open the sandwich slightly to check that the cheese has melted sufficiently. If not, reduce the heat to low and leave the sandwich in the pan a little longer, until it has.

Repeat to grill the second sandwich. Serve and enjoy.

Lunch   Level ①⟨2⟩✦3✦

Pink Oyster Lobster Rolls

Makes 2

1 teaspoon olive oil

9oz (250g) pink oyster mushrooms, coarsely torn (regular oyster mushrooms work well, too)

1 tablespoon lemon juice

½ celery rib, finely chopped

Small bunch chives, finely chopped

½ teaspoon nori flakes

¼ cup (60ml) Ten-Second Mayo (see page 262), or store-bought vegan mayo

2 tablespoons Vegan Butter (see page 272), or store-bought vegan butter, at room temperature

2 large hotdog buns, sliced from the top down

6 lettuce leaves

Handful of ridged potato chips

Sea salt and freshly ground black pepper

Someone once told me I look like Richard Dreyfus in *Jaws*. In retrospect, I think it was supposed to be an insult, but I have no issue with looking like an East Coast, renegade marine-biologist with something to prove. In fact, let me complete the picture for you as I don an adorable bucket hat while posing with this New England-style lobster roll: Halloween costume and lunch sorted in one! I've used pink oyster mushrooms to create the shellfish illusion and I've added all the ingredients of a traditional lobster roll to complete the scene. Finish with a little nori seaweed to boost the seafood flavor and you might as well be enjoying the sunset on a pier in Martha's Vineyard! I think we're gonna need a bigger napkin.

Place a frying pan over medium-low heat. Add the oil and swirl to coat. Add half the pink oyster mushrooms, making sure the pan isn't too crowded. Season with salt and pepper and fry for 2 minutes on each side, or until just cooked. If using pink oyster mushrooms, they will lose their pink color but should turn a deep orange, similar to cooked lobster.

Remove from the pan and allow to cool fully. Repeat with the other half of the mushrooms.

Transfer the mushrooms to the fridge to chill for at least 15 minutes.

Place the chilled mushrooms in a bowl and add the lemon juice, celery, chives, nori, and vegan mayo. Stir gently to combine.

Butter the buns and add the lettuce leaves. Pack in the mushroom filling and wedge in a few chips.

Serve with vegan slaw (for homemade, see page 65), ketchup, and more chips on the side.

Mushroom Brisket Sandwiches

Makes 2

For the mushroom brisket
12oz (350g) (around 4 large) king oyster mushrooms
3 tablespoons vegetable oil
1 tablespoon smoked paprika
1 teaspoon garlic powder
½ teaspoon onion powder
½ teaspoon English mustard powder
Pinch cayenne pepper
1 teaspoon vegan beef bouillon powder
1 teaspoon light brown sugar
Sea salt flakes and freshly ground black pepper

For the slaw
¾ cup (50g) shredded red cabbage
¾ cup (50g) shredded white cabbage
1 teaspoon lemon juice
3 tablespoons Ten-Second Mayo (see page 262), or store-bought vegan mayo

For the sandwiches
2 large white sandwich buns
2 tablespoons soft Vegan Butter (see page 272), or store-bought vegan butter
6 gherkin slices
¼ cup (60ml) Gochujang Barbecue Sauce (see page 265), or store-bought vegan barbecue sauce
½ onion, sliced in rings

Did you hear that? It was the sound of every barbecue pitmaster in America collectively having a little cry over this utterly irresistible sandwich. They're upset because it's made out of mushrooms and they're a bit scared of change. But, don't worry, a single bite of this big boy will cheer them right up. It's smoky, meaty, and packs an umami punch like a brisket sandwich should. If that doesn't put a smile on everybody's face, I don't know what will.

To make the brisket, place the king oyster mushrooms in a large bowl and add 2 tablespoons of the vegetable oil. Massage it into the mushrooms carefully, making sure they're all evenly coated.

In a small bowl, whisk together the spices, bouillon, brown sugar, 1 teaspoon salt, and ½ teaspoon pepper. Sprinkle over the mushrooms and gently rub it in.

Place a large cast-iron frying pan over medium heat and add the remaining 1 tablespoon oil. Once the pan is very hot, add the mushrooms side by side and sprinkle with more sea salt flakes.

Using a heavy-bottomed saucepan or a pan lid, press down on the mushrooms until they sizzle. Keep the mushrooms pressed for 2 minutes, until their juices start to be released. Remove the press and flip the mushrooms. Repeat the process to press the second side.

Flip the mushrooms again and reduce the heat to medium-low. Stop pressing the mushrooms and cook them for another 5–8 minutes on each side.

Use a fork to check that the stems of the mushrooms are soft and fully cooked through. If they're not, press the mushrooms again and cook for a few minutes more.

Once fully cooked and charred on both sides, remove the mushrooms from the pan. Use 2 forks to shred the mushrooms, then return them to the frying pan (off the heat) to keep warm.

In a small bowl, combine the slaw ingredients, add a pinch of salt, and mix well.

To make the sandwiches, slice the buns and butter both sides, then divide the slaw and gherkins between 2 of the halves. Top with the mushroom brisket, barbecue sauce, and onion, then add the tops of the buns and serve.

Couldn't be Cozier French Onion Soup

☺ x 2

5 ½ tablespoons (80g) Vegan Butter (see page 272), or store-bought vegan butter

1½lb (650g) onions, finely chopped

1 teaspoon sugar

1 tablespoon all-purpose flour

7oz (200ml) vegan dry white wine

3 cups (700ml) boiling vegetable stock

1 tablespoon Marmite

Leaves of 6 thyme sprigs

½ cup (120g) Vegan Mozzarella (see page 252), or vegan melting cheese

4 slices baguette

Freshly ground black pepper

Something happens to me when I'm cuddled on the couch with a bowl of soup. Like a hibernating Pokémon, I evolve into my final form. I become some kind of elegant mammalian slug with a barely perceptible heart rate and a look of sheer bliss permanently on my face. What can I say, it's my happy place, and I can think of nobody I'd rather share it with than this bowl of vegan French onion soup.

Place a medium, heavy-bottomed saucepan for which you have a lid over medium-low heat and add the butter. Once melted, add the onions.

Fry for 10 minutes, or until softened, covering with the lid but stirring occasionally. Add the sugar and stir to combine, then fry for 10–15 minutes more, or until soft, browned, and caramelized. Don't let the onions burn.

Add the flour and stir well to combine. Continue stirring as you gradually pour in the white wine, boiling stock, and Marmite. Stir and bring to a simmer, add two-thirds of the thyme, then cover with the lid again and leave to cook for 20 minutes.

When ready to serve, preheat the broiler. Divide the soup between 2 large ovenproof bowls. Divide the vegan cheese between the slices of baguette and float on top of the bowls of soup. Place under the broiler until the cheese is melted and golden brown, around 5 minutes.

Sprinkle with the remaining thyme and a little pepper, then serve.

Blind Scouse

☺ x 4

½ cup (90g) pearl barley
1 tablespoon Vegan Butter
    (see page 272), or store-
    bought vegan butter
1 onion, chopped
2 garlic cloves, crushed or
    finely grated
2 celery ribs, chopped
2 large carrots, chopped
    into large chunks
1 tablespoon brown rice
    miso paste
2 teaspoons English
    mustard
2 tablespoons all-purpose
    flour
4 cups (1 liter) vegetable
    stock
14oz (400g) new potatoes
3 bay leaves
2 thyme sprigs
2 rosemary sprigs
Sea salt and freshly ground
    black pepper

I was born in Liverpool, so, naturally, the local dish of scouse was a huge part of my childhood. Mam would whack a huge potful on the stove at the start of almost every week and we'd eat it with "cobs" of bread and pickled cabbage or beets. Each day, she'd replenish the leftovers with fresh veggies and the process would repeat. Scouse is a super-old, chunky sailor's stew that varies from family to family, but was traditionally made with beef or lamb. Back in the day, poorer families (like Mam's) that could rarely afford meat used to make "blind scouse," which was a vegan variation. It's probably one of the first vegan dishes I ever (unknowingly) ate, and it still hits the spot for me every time.

Place a medium saucepan over medium heat and half-fill it with water. Bring to a boil, then add the pearl barley. Reduce to a simmer until the barley is swollen and tender, around 10 minutes.

While the barley cooks, place a large saucepan or cast-iron casserole dish for which you have a lid over medium heat. Add the butter and onion. Sauté for a few minutes before adding the garlic. Continue to cook for 1 minute more, but don't let the garlic burn.

Add the celery and carrots and fry for 2 minutes before stirring in the brown rice miso paste, mustard, and flour.

Pour in the stock, stirring well, until no lumps of flour remain. Add the potatoes and herbs, then cover with the lid and bring to a simmer.

After 20 minutes of simmering, test a potato with a fork. If cooked, remove the pan from the heat; if not, cover and simmer for another 5–10 minutes. (This recipe is designed to simmer for a while, so don't worry about overcooking it.)

Drain the barley and add it to the scouse. Stir well and season with salt and pepper.

Serve topped with pickled, shredded beets or red cabbage and with a side of warm crusty bread.

Miss Silky's Instant Mac 'n' Cheese

☺ x 2

For the instant mac mix

4 tablespoons nutritional yeast

4 tablespoons tapioca flour

1 tablespoon cornstarch

1 teaspoon onion powder

1 teaspoon garlic salt

1 teaspoon English mustard powder

1 teaspoon vegan lactic acid powder (optional)

Sea salt

For the mac 'n' cheese

5oz (150g) vegan pasta (not egg pasta!)

1½ cups (350ml) any plant milk (soy milk works best)

1½ tablespoons Vegan Butter (see page 272), or store-bought vegan butter

This is one of those pastas you come across during a late-night scroll through the depths of Instagram's "strangely satisfying" feed. It is the kind of pasta you find among pictures of perfectly neon slime and videos of stuff being slowly squished by pneumatic crushers. Why? Because it's perfect! Just look at how glossy that sauce is, gently clinging to the pasta. It's also insanely easy to make, as well as being super silky. Speaking of silky, this recipe is named after Miss Silky, who happens to be my childhood comfort blanket. She's the only thing I've ever come across which is more silky than this mac 'n' cheese, so I slapped her name on it. Love you, Miss Silky.

Place all the ingredients for the instant mac mix into a blender with ¼ teaspoon salt and pulse-blend until the mixture is finely powdered. Remove from the blender and store in an airtight jar for up to 6 months.

To make the mac 'n' cheese, boil the pasta in a saucepan of well salted water, according to the instructions on the package.

In a separate saucepan, combine the plant milk with 3 tablespoons of the instant mac mix. Whisk well, then place over medium-low heat.

Whisk constantly until the sauce thickens dramatically, then add the vegan butter and mix through until melted and fully combined.

Drain the pasta and add it to the sauce. Stir to combine, then serve.

Seitan Reuben

Makes 1

Full transparency: this is the reason I included deli meat in the Building Block Recipes section of this book (see page 245). A proper Manhattan-style reuben is something I've always wanted to try, to the point that I once stood in Katz's Deli in New York for a full thirty minutes, silently watching how the staff made them, before ordering a side of garlic pickles in case they called security.

For the Russian dressing
½ shallot, very finely chopped
¼ cup (60ml) Ten-Second Mayo (see page 262), or store-bought vegan mayo
1 tablespoon ketchup
1 teaspoon vegan horseradish sauce
1 teaspoon hot sauce
2 teaspoons sweet cucumber relish
1 teaspoon vegan Worcestershire sauce (I use mushroom ketchup or Henderson's Relish)
Pinch paprika
Fine sea salt

For the sandwich
1 quantity Seitan Deli Meat (see page 245, and see recipe note, right), or 3½oz (100g) store-bought vegan deli meat
2 slices of soft rye bread (not the firm, dark German style)
3 tablespoons sauerkraut
3 slices store-bought vegan smoky/Swiss cheese
1 tablespoon Vegan Butter (see page 272), or store-bought vegan butter
Gherkin or dill pickle, to serve

For the dressing, place the shallot in a mortar and pestle and crush to a coarse paste. Transfer to a bowl, add the remaining dressing ingredients, with a pinch of salt and, stir to combine.

To make the sandwich, using your sharpest knife, cut 10–12 very thin slices of deli meat.

Lay the slices of bread on a cutting board and spread both with the Russian dressing. Top 1 slice with the seitan deli meat, sauerkraut, and cheese, then cover with the second slice of bread.

Spread the whole outside of the sandwich with the vegan butter. Place a cast-iron frying pan over medium-low heat until the pan is hot. Place the sandwich in the pan and use a heavy lid or separate pan to weigh down the top. Cook for 3–5 minutes, making sure the bread doesn't burn, then flip and repeat on the other side.

Remove from the pan, slice in half, and serve with a gherkin on the side, and maybe some fries.

> **Recipe note**
> If you're making everything from scratch, be sure to make the deli meat the day before, even though it appears halfway down the ingredients list. It takes some time, but is well worth it.

Tofish Finger Sammy

Makes 1

For the marinade (optional)
1 tablespoon vegan fish
    sauce, or light soy sauce
½ tablespoon lemon juice
½ tablespoon caper brine
⅛ teaspoon nori flakes

For the tofish fingers
5oz (140g) extra-firm tofu,
    drained
¼ cup (60g) bread crumbs
½ teaspoon smoked paprika
¼ teaspoon garlic powder
¼ cup (60g) cornstarch
⅓ cup (100ml) any plant milk
    (soy milk works best)
2 teaspoons lemon juice
¼ cup (60ml) vegetable oil
Fine sea salt and freshly
    ground black pepper

For the sandwich
2 tablespoons Ten-Second
    Mayo (see page 262), or
    store-bought vegan mayo
1 teaspoon ketchup
1 teaspoon sriracha
1 gherkin, finely chopped
2 slices thick white bread
2 gem or romaine lettuce
    leaves

My dad knows how to make one single dish: a fish finger (aka fish stick) sandwich. He's vegan now, so that recipe no longer sees the light of day, but it has a special place in my mouth-memory. As a kid, the best thing about dad's fish finger sandwich was that his quantities were way off! Way too many fish fingers coated in way too much sauce on bread that was literally too thick to get in my mouth: absolute heaven! My vegan take uses tofu instead of fish, which you can marinate for more flavor (if you have time). But, honestly, there's so much sauce and seasoning in this sandwich that flavor is the last thing you'll be searching for.

In a small bowl, whisk together all the marinade ingredients, if using. Set aside.

Slice the tofu into 4 fish finger-sized oblongs and wrap in paper towels. Press down gently to absorb any excess moisture.

If you're marinating the tofu, use a small, sharp knife to score the tofu, almost like the flakes of a piece of fish, all the way down the length of each piece. Don't cut too deep into the tofu or it'll fall apart. Place the tofu in the marinade, cover and place in the fridge for a minimum of 3 hours. Once marinated, remove the tofu from the fridge and set aside.

Preheat the oven to 350°F (180°C) convection.

Take 3 small mixing bowls. In bowl 1 mix together the bread crumbs, paprika, ½ teaspoon salt, ⅛ teaspoon pepper, and the garlic powder. In bowl 2 place the cornstarch. In bowl 3 whisk together the plant milk and the lemon juice.

Working with 1 finger of tofu at a time, coat in the cornstarch, then the plant milk, then back in the cornstarch, back in the plant milk and finally in the bread crumbs. Repeat to coat all the fingers.

Arrange the tofu fingers on a lined baking sheet and drizzle with the vegetable oil on both sides. Place in the oven for 35 minutes, flipping the fingers halfway.

To make the sandwich, in a small bowl, mix together the mayo, ketchup, sriracha, and gherkin. Spread most of this on a slice of white bread and stack with the lettuce leaves.

Top with the tofish fingers straight from the oven, drizzle with the remaining sauce and sandwich with the second slice of bread. Serve hot with ridged potato chips, if you like.

Lunch Level ① ② ✦

Shaved Tofu Doner

Makes 2

For the shaved tofu

7oz (200g) block extra-firm tofu, drained
1 small onion, chopped
1 tablespoon dark soy sauce
1 tablespoon liquid smoke
2 tablespoons vegetable oil
1½ teaspoons garlic powder
1 teaspoon dried oregano
2 teaspoons ground cumin
2 teaspoons ground cilantro
¼ teaspoon ground cinnamon
2 teaspoons light brown sugar
2 teaspoons potato flour
⅓ cup (100ml) water
Fine sea salt and freshly ground black pepper

For the rest

2 large pitas, split and warmed
4 tablespoons Zankou Garlic Whip (see page 266), or vegan, store-bought garlic mayo, plus more to serve
¼ red cabbage, shredded
½ gem lettuce, shredded
½ red onion, finely sliced
¼ cucumber, finely sliced
1 tomato, sliced
Hot sauce (optional)

Even though I've been doing this for years, some recipes are still a huge surprise when they work. The plan with this guy was to try to shave the tofu with a cheese slice or mandoline, to get nice, thin, meaty curls that resemble doner meat, without a big fuss. Turns out, it worked perfectly and I won the Nobel Peace Prize. Huzzah! Once coated in my spiced marinade, packed with all the flavors of doner meat, then grilled, the tofu picks up a deliciously meaty texture with crispy caramelized edges. Just be sure to use extra-firm tofu, or it won't hold its shape when shaved.

Use a mandoline or cheese slicer to shave the tofu into thin strips, about ⅛in (3mm) thick. Carefully lay them on a nonstick baking sheet.

Place the remaining tofu ingredients in a blender with 1 teaspoon salt and ½ teaspoon pepper and blend until very smooth. Use a pastry brush to baste the tofu strips with the blended marinade.

Preheat the broiler and place the strips of tofu under the broiler. Broil until lightly browned, around 5 minutes, before flipping, basting again and repeating on the other side.

Once the tofu is lightly crisped on the edges and has taken on a slightly meatier texture, remove from under the broiler.

Spread the inside of the warmed pitas with the Zankou Garlic Whip. Stuff each with half the cabbage, lettuce, onion, cucumber, tomato, and tofu.

Serve with extra garlic whip and plenty of hot sauce, if you like.

Tuna Melt

Makes 2

2oz (50g) TVP strips or curls

2in (5cm) piece of kombu

6 tablespoons Ten-Second Mayo (see page 262), or store-bought vegan mayo

½ celery rib, finely chopped

1 tablespoon lemon juice

½ teaspoon Dijon mustard

½ shallot, finely chopped

1 large gherkin, finely chopped

4 teaspoons Vegan Butter (see page 272), or store-bought vegan butter, at room temperature

4 thick slices white bread

4 tablespoons Vegan Mozzarella (see page 252), or store-bought vegan melting cheese

Sea salt and freshly ground black pepper

If you were a vegetarian student in the 1990s or 2000s, then you may be suffering from TVP PTSD. Textured vegetable protein has been something of a workhorse ingredient in student dorms around the world for literally decades, thanks to its low price point and ability to somehow make a depressing veggie bolognese even sadder. But, I'm still a massive fan of TVP; I just think we need to get creative with how we use it. Here, TVP strips or curls become a vegan tuna sub. Once hydrated and shredded, the flaky texture is mind-blowingly similar and ideal for a cheesy, melting, grilled sandwich.

Place the TVP and kombu in a bowl and cover with just-boiled water. Cover and leave to rehydrate for 10 minutes, then drain well and remove and discard the kombu.

Transfer the TVP to a nut-milk bag or piece of muslin. Gather the sides and twist firmly to squeeze out the excess moisture. Unwrap and rub the drained TVP through your fingers to break it into tuna-like flakes. Depending on the size of your TVP pieces, you may need to use a knife to cut them into smaller flakes.

In a bowl, stir together the TVP tuna, mayo, celery, lemon juice, mustard, shallot, gherkin, ¼ teaspoon salt, and ½ teaspoon pepper.

Preheat the broiler. Butter the pieces of bread on both sides. Divide the tuna mayo between 2 slices and top with the vegan cheese. Place the loaded slices under the broiler until melted and bubbling. Remove from under the broiler.

Heat a frying pan or grill pan over medium heat. Sandwich the tuna and cheese slices with their second pieces of bread and place on the hot pan. Press down with a pan lid and allow to toast. Carefully flip the sandwiches and toast on the other side.

Serve with fries or chips.

Kimchi Fried-Rice Waffles

Makes 5–6

2¼ cups (400g) cooked rice
  (sushi, jasmine, or sticky
  rice work best)
7oz (200g) vegan kimchi,
  coarsely chopped
1 tablespoon soy sauce
1 tablespoon toasted
  sesame oil
½ teaspoon sushi seasoning
  (or see recipe introduction)
2 tablespoons rice flour
1 tablespoon vegetable oil,
  or nonstick spray oil
  (see recipe introduction)
2 scallions, sliced or
  shredded
2 teaspoons toasted
  black-sesame seeds
Sriracha, to serve
Shredded nori, to serve
Vegan Fried Eggs (see page
  36), to serve (optional)

Equipment needed
Waffle maker (optional)

I'm a total fan of bibimbap from Korean restaurants. It comes served in hot-stone bowls called a dolsot that makes the bottom layer of rice all crispy, and I'm all about the crisp. I don't have a massive hot-stone bowl at home, so I embarked on an adventure with some leftover sushi rice to find an alternative route to crispy rice heaven. I fired up my waffle maker and, after a few sticky disasters, this guy popped out! If you don't have a waffle maker, you can easily do this in a lightly oiled frying pan instead; just be sure to flip the rice "pancake" to fry both sides. A heads-up: you're going to want to grease up your waffle iron really well with vegetable oil before making each fried rice waffle, ideally with nonstick spray oil, if you have some. Otherwise, sticky rice by name, sticky rice by nature! If you can't find sushi seasoning, you can make your own (see page 85).

In a bowl, mix together the cooked rice, vegan kimchi, soy sauce, sesame oil, sushi seasoning, and rice flour.

Heat a waffle iron (or see recipe introduction and use a frying pan) and brush well with vegetable oil or nonstick spray oil. Fill a cup measure with the rice mixture and turn it out into the center of the hot waffle iron. Close and cook for at least 5 minutes.

Open the waffle iron and carefully remove the waffle. Repeat the process to wafflify the remaining rice mixture.

Top the waffles with the scallions, black sesame seeds, sriracha, and nori, and/or one of my vegan fried eggs.

Creamy Caper Tater Salad

☺ x 4–6

1½ lb (680g) new potatoes
1 shallot, halved and finely
  sliced
½ cup (120ml) Ten-Second
  Mayo (see page 262), or
  store-bought vegan mayo
1 tablespoon Dijon mustard
3 tablespoons capers,
  drained
10–20 cornichons, chopped
Small bunch dill, finely
  chopped
Small bunch chives, finely
  chopped
Sea salt flakes and freshly
  ground black pepper

Nothing says summer carb-ecue like a creamy potato salad. Decent vegan mayo is vital, of course, but the taste joy is all about texture. New potatoes are a must, for that gentle bite, but I also demand that you include my best pal: the cornichon. It delivers a crunch, some tang, and a salty lift that I'd be heartbroken without.

Heat a large saucepan of salted water over medium heat until boiling. Add the new potatoes and boil until fork-tender (around 15 minutes).

Drain the potatoes and submerge them in a bowl of very cold water to stop them from cooking (if the water becomes warm, drain it and top off with cold water again).

In a large bowl, mix together the remaining ingredients; add a pinch of salt and ¼ teaspoon pepper.

When the potatoes are cold, drain thoroughly and add to the mayo dressing. Toss to coat and serve.

Level ①②③

Forbidden Rice Poke Bowl with Beet Salmon

☺ x 2

For the salmon

4 large golden beets, scrubbed

3 teaspoons vegetable oil

2 cups (500ml) boiling water

3in (7.5cm) piece of kombu (or 2 nori sheets, coarsely torn)

2 tablespoons red or white miso paste

Juice 1 lemon

2 teaspoons red beet powder (or 1 small fresh beet, coarsely grated)

2 tablespoons mirin

Fine sea salt

For the rice

1½ cups (300g) forbidden rice (aka black rice), washed and drained

1½ cups (350ml) water

3 tablespoons rice vinegar

1½ teaspoons sugar

For the toppings

½ cucumber, finely sliced or peeled into strips

1 avocado, peeled, pitted, and sliced

Small bunch pea shoots (optional)

1 teaspoon black sesame seeds

Soy sauce, sriracha, or vegan mayo, to serve

Ask any English dad named Keith how he feels about black rice and poke bowls and you'll get the same answer: they're a trend. But here's why Keith owes the world a very sincere YouTube apology and corresponding Instagram statement of regret. Black rice originated in China about ten thousand years ago and poke has been served by Hawaiian fishermen for absolutely ever. That's about as far from a quick fidget-spinner, flash-in-the-pan trend as you can get. Obviously, my version doesn't contain fish, so we're deviating from but, where possible, I've tried to keep things simple, classic, and delicious.

To make the salmon, preheat the oven to 350F (180C) convection. Gently prick the golden beets with a fork and rub with the vegetable oil. Wrap each beet individually in foil. Place on a baking sheet and bake for 45 minutes.

Once cooked, remove from the oven and allow to cool fully without unwrapping.

To make the marinade, in a bowl, mix the remaining salmon ingredients with 1 teaspoon salt. When the beets are cool enough to handle, use a teaspoon to gently remove the outer skin (it should come off easily). Slice the cooked, peeled beets into ½in (1.5cm) cubes and transfer them to the bowl with the marinade.

Cover and place in the fridge to marinate for a minimum of 2 hours, or, ideally, overnight.

Place the rice in a medium saucepan for which you have a tight-fitting lid and cover with the water. Bring to a boil over medium heat. As soon as the rice boils, reduce the heat to the lowest your stove allows and cover with the lid. Leave to simmer for 20 minutes, then turn off the heat and leave it there to steam for 10 minutes: do not be tempted to lift the lid!

Once cooked, use a spatula to spread the cooked rice onto a baking sheet to cool.

To make your sushi seasoning, in a small bowl, whisk together the rice vinegar, sugar, and 1 teaspoon salt until the salt and sugar are dissolved. While the rice is cooling, sprinkle with the sushi seasoning and mix well to combine. Set aside to cool fully.

Divide the cooked rice, salmon and vegetable toppings between 2 bowls. Finish with the sesame seeds and serve with soy sauce, sriracha, or vegan mayo.

Tuna Niçoise Salad

☺ x 4

For the tuna

1in (2.5cm) piece of kombu
2 cups (500ml) boiling water
2oz (65g) TVP chunks
2 tablespoons vegan fish
    sauce, or soy sauce
2 tablespoons extra virgin
    olive oil
1 teaspoon rice vinegar
Sea salt and freshly ground
    black pepper

For the boiled eggs

10½oz (300g) silken tofu
2 teaspoons agar agar powder
3 tablespoons water
½ teaspoon kala namak
    (black salt)
4–6 tablespoons "If It Ain't
    Yolk" Sauce (see page 269)

For the dressing

⅔ cup (150ml) extra-virgin
    olive oil
¼ cup (50ml) lemon juice
1 tablespoon wholegrain
    mustard
2 teaspoons agave syrup,
    or sugar
¼ teaspoon nori flakes

For the salad

14oz (400g) new potatoes
5½oz (150g) green beans
½ cucumber, cut into
    ¼in (5mm) wedges
2 tomatoes, each cut into
    8 slices
2 tablespoons capers, drained
½ x 14oz (400g) can of mixed
    beans, drained and rinsed

Equipment needed

High-speed blender (optional)
Silicone egg mold

I've already professed my undying love for TVP as a tuna substitute, back in my Tuna Melt recipe (see page 79), so I'm going to shift the spotlight momentarily to my vegan boiled egg recipe. They're simply made from silken tofu, blended until smooth and reset in an egg mold using agar agar (a vegan substitute for gelatine). Once cooled, I scoop out the center, fill with "If It Ain't Yolk" Sauce (see page 269) and return to the fridge to set. Imagine the gasps from your pals when the only vegan at the summer party unveils a salad packed with glossy tuna flakes and perfectly soft-boiled eggs! Now bask in that spotlight, bask, I say!

To make the tuna, place the kombu in a bowl and add the boiling water. Stir in the TVP and cover. Leave for at least 1 hour, or ideally overnight.

Drain the TVP and discard the kombu. Transfer the TVP to a nut-milk bag or piece of muslin or cheesecloth and wring out excess moisture. Transfer to a bowl and, with your fingers, break it into rough flakes. Add the fish sauce, olive oil, rice vinegar, and a pinch of salt. Massage with your fingertips until combined and the mixture resembles tuna flakes. Set aside.

For the eggs, place the tofu, agar agar, and water into a high-speed blender. Blend until very smooth. Or place the ingredients in a tall container or bowl and blend with an immersion blender until very smooth. Transfer to a small pan and place over low heat.

Stirring with a silicone spatula, bring to a very gentle boil. Stir for 2–3 minutes, or until thickened slightly, then turn off the heat and stir in the kala namak. Working quickly, divide the mixture between 4 wells in a silicone egg mold, smooth the surface and chill to set for at least 1 hour.

Use a teaspoon measure or melon baller to remove circular, yolk-sized holes from the center of the egg whites. Fill with the "If It Ain't Yolk" Sauce and return to the fridge to set for at least another hour, or up to 48 hours.

To make the dressing, place all the ingredients in a clean jam jar and screw on the lid. Shake well until combined, then season.

Place a saucepan of salted boiling water over medium heat. Boil the potatoes for 15 minutes, until fork-tender. Use a slotted spoon to remove them and plunge into a bowl of cold water to stop them from cooking. Repeat with the green beans, boiling them for 3–5 minutes, then draining and plunging into the water.

Arrange the cucumber, tomatoes, capers, mixed beans, cooked potatoes, and green beans in a large salad bowl and dress lightly with the dressing. Top with the tuna and boiled eggs and sprinkle with pepper to serve.

Lunch

Level ①②✴

Grandma's Chicken Saaaalad

😊 x 4

For the salad
2 fillets (12 ½oz/350g) Seitan Chicken (see page 235)
1 tablespoon olive oil
2 heads romaine lettuce, torn

For the croutons
100g sourdough bread, roughly torn
1 tablespoon olive oil
¼ teaspoon garlic granules
Sea salt flakes and freshly ground black pepper

For the dressing
1 garlic clove
1 tablespoon capers, finely chopped
¼ teaspoon nori flakes
1 tablespoon oil from a jar of sundried tomatoes
3 pitted green olives, very finely chopped
2 tablespoons lemon juice
1½ tablespoons (20g) vegan Parmesan, finely grated
½ teaspoon Dijon mustard
6 tablespoons vegan mayo

Vegan

Agony Aunt

Anchovies! How do you replace them on pizzas and in sauces?
Finely mince together
½ teaspoon sea salt flakes,
1 tablespoon capers,
¼ teaspoon nori flakes,
1 tablespoon oil from a jar of sundried tomatoes, and
3 very finely chopped pitted green olives. Bingo!

No, my grandma never actually made this salad, but if you think this millennial is going to let a book go to press without a *Friends* reference, you've got another thing coming! My Seitan Chicken (see page 235) is the shining star of this salad, so I've not suggested using an alternative in the recipe. If you have a store-bought chicken alternative you already love, then by all means make the sub!

Preheat the oven to 400°F (200°C) convection. Rub the seitan chicken with the olive oil and place on a baking sheet. Set aside.

Place the lettuce in a large serving bowl.

For the croutons, place the torn sourdough in a bowl. Drizzle with the oil and sprinkle with the garlic granules, a pinch of salt, and a few good grinds of pepper. Toss to combine, then spread out on the baking sheet with the seitan.

Place the sheet in the preheated oven to bake for 10 minutes.

Remove the croutons when golden brown and crispy, leaving the chicken to bake for 10 minutes more, or until browned.

Slice the chicken into strips, or pull apart into curls, and add to the serving bowl with the lettuce. Top with the croutons.

To make the dressing, crush the garlic with the flat side of a knife on a cutting board, then sprinkle with ½ teaspoon sea salt flakes. Drag the knife across the garlic until you've created a smooth paste. Put the garlic paste into a small bowl with the remaining dressing ingredients and ¼ teaspoon pepper and whisk together.

Drizzle half the dressing over the salad and toss well. Top the tossed salad with more Parmesan and serve with the remaining dressing on the side.

Crispy Tofu Salmon with Beets and Lentils

☺ x 2

For the salad

18oz (500g) vacuum-packed cooked beets, quartered

14oz (400g) can beluga lentils, drained

1 tablespoon lemon juice, plus more to serve

Small bunch dill or chives, finely chopped

Small bunch parsley leaves, finely chopped

¼ cup (60ml) Ten-Second Mayo (see page 262), or store-bought vegan mayo

1 tablespoon wholegrain mustard

2 teaspoons capers

For the salmon

14oz (400g) firm tofu

1 tablespoon beet juice (from the vacuum-pack)

1⅔ cups (400ml) water

2 tablespoons lemon juice

2 tablespoons vegan fish sauce, or light soy sauce

1 nori sheet

1 sheet rice paper, or 1 spring roll wrapper

7oz (200ml) water

2 tablespoons potato flour

2 tablespoons vegetable oil

Fine sea salt

Honestly, is there anything our reigning queen tofu can't do? All right, she can't bring back your ex, but he had problematic opinions about S Club 7 anyway, and we all know that's a big red flag parade. I'm talking about the absolute versatility of tofu! The sheer nerve it takes to turn up to a party looking like a crispy salmon fillet... she's got range and, yes, we love a versatile plant protein queen.

Toss together all the salad ingredients in a bowl. Cover and place in the fridge.

To make the salmon, drain the tofu and carefully squeeze out as much moisture as you can without breaking up the structure of the tofu. Slice it into 2 5½ x 2in (14 x 5cm) fillets.

To make the tofu resemble flaky fish, place a chopstick on either side of a tofu fillet and use a sharp knife to score partway through the fillet repeatedly until you've scored down the entire length.

In a deep dish, mix together the beet juice, water, lemon juice, and vegan fish sauce or soy sauce with 2 teaspoons salt. Submerge the tofu fillets in the marinade and leave to marinate for at least 1 hour. Drain and pat the tofu dry with paper towels.

Slice the nori and rice paper each into 2 rectangles the same size as the top of the tofu fillets. Lay the nori rectangles over the tofu fillets. Fill a shallow bowl with the water and whisk in the potato flour. Dip the rice papers in this mixture for a few seconds, or until just softened, then lay them on top of the nori.

Use a pastry brush to brush the remaining potato flour mixture over the exposed parts of the tofu fillets.

Heat a large frying pan over medium heat and add the vegetable oil. When hot, place the tofu fillets in the pan, rice-paper side down first, and fry until crispy and browned, around 2 minutes. Flip and fry the bottoms for 2 minutes more, then repeat on each side of the tofu.

Serve the cooked tofu on the salad with an extra squeeze of lemon juice.

Seared Shroom Bossam

☺ x 4

For the sauce

3 tablespoons ssamjang
   (Korean fermented soy
   bean paste)
1 tablespoon gochujang
4 tablespoons toasted
   sesame oil
4 tablespoons rice vinegar

For the shrooms

1 tablespoon doenjang
5 scallions, white parts
   only, coarsely chopped
⅜in (1cm) piece ginger,
   peeled and coarsely
   chopped
3 garlic cloves, peeled
1 teaspoon light brown sugar
Pinch ground aniseed
2 tablespoons water
14oz (400g) oyster
   mushroom cluster
   (the larger the better)
Sea salt flakes

To serve

7oz (200g) vegan kimchi
Steamed rice
3–4 small heads lettuce
   (baby gem, bibb, or baby
   cos work well)

Bossam is a Korean dish traditionally involving shredded, spiced pork, but we're using insanely delicious hunks of seared oyster mushrooms instead. Each diner takes a lettuce leaf, fills it with sliced shrooms, rice, kimchi, and ssamjang sauce in what can only be described as a rather handsy feeding frenzy. It's a perfect dish for bringing people together.

To make the sauce, place all the ingredients in a small bowl and whisk well to combine.

For the shrooms, place everything except the mushrooms in a blender with ½ teaspoon salt and blend until smooth. This is your searing sauce; don't confuse it with the ssam sauce, which is for serving.

Place a medium-sized frying pan over medium heat. When hot, add the mushroom cluster: it should hiss immediately. Weigh down the mushroom cluster with a heavy lid or separate cast-iron pan. Fry for 5 minutes before removing the press and flipping. Weigh down the mushrooms again and fry for another 5 minutes.

Once fried on both sides, brush the cluster with the searing sauce from the blender and cook again on both sides for a few minutes more, until the mushroom cluster is fragrant and smoky.

Remove the cluster from the pan and place on a cutting board. Slice it into shreds with a sharp knife.

To serve, place the hot, seared mushrooms in the center of the table and surround with the kimchi, the bowl of ssam sauce, steamed rice, and lettuce.

Hold a lettuce leaf in your hand and stack with some of each ingredient. Wrap the lettuce up and enjoy.

Nachos Pretending to be Fattoush

☺ x 4

For everyone who still thinks salad is boring, I present to you: salad in drag! This plate of nachos has tumbled headfirst into the dress-up box and come out dressed as a plate of fattoush (already arguably the best salad out there). We've gone big with the pieces of crispy pita to emulate tortilla chips and we've dressed everything in a tangy, lemony dressing. It's miles from the traditional Levantine fattoush, but sometimes that's what it takes to become America's Next Drag Salad-Star!

For the pita chips

5 pita breads, split

2 tablespoons olive oil

⅛ teaspoon Aleppo pepper, or regular chili flakes

¼ teaspoon ground cumin

1 teaspoon light brown sugar

Sea salt flakes

For the salad

½ red onion, finely sliced

Juice 1 lemon

3 ripe tomatoes, cut into large chunks

1 cucumber, cut into large chunks

6 radishes, finely sliced

2 small heads lettuce, sliced (romaine or baby gem work well)

Small bunch mint, leaves coarsely torn

Small bunch parsley, leaves coarsely torn

1 quantity Zankou Garlic Whip (see page 266), or store-bought vegan garlic mayo

¼ cup (45g) pomegranate seeds

A few pickled green chilies

For the dressing

3 tablespoons lemon juice

2 tablespoons pomegranate molasses

1 garlic clove, crushed or finely grated

2 teaspoons red wine vinegar

½ cup (120ml) extra-virgin olive oil

2 teaspoons ground sumac

To make the pita chips, preheat the oven to 325F (160C) convection.

Slice the pita bread into triangles about the size of tortilla chips. Place in a large bowl, drizzle with the olive oil, and toss to coat. Sprinkle with the spices, sugar, and 1 teaspoon salt, then arrange on a baking sheet in a single layer. Bake for 20 minutes, flipping the chips halfway through. Remove from the oven and allow to cool.

For the salad, in a small bowl, combine the red onion and lemon juice. Cover and place in the fridge to quick-pickle for a minimum of 10 minutes.

In a bowl, combine the remaining salad vegetables and herbs and toss to mix.

Put all the dressing ingredients in a jar and seal the lid. Shake well until combined.

Add the dressing to the salad and toss to coat. Drain the pickled red onions.

On a large plate or salad bowl, arrange a layer of the pita chips. Top with some of the dressed salad, half the quick-pickled onions, and half the garlic whip. Repeat the process, layering as you go.

Finish with the pomegranate seeds and the pickled chilies.

Cannellini Gnocchi with Pesto

☺ × 2

For the gnocchi
2 x 14oz (400g) cans
    cannellini beans
1¾ cups (200g) all-purpose
    flour, plus more to dust
Fine sea salt and freshly
    ground black pepper

For the pesto
⅓ cup (50g) pine nuts
1⅔ cup (100g) basil,
    coarsely chopped
½ cup (60g) Grateable
    Parmesan (see page 255),
    or store-bought vegan
    Parmesan, finely grated,
    plus more to serve
⅔ cup (150ml) extra-virgin
    olive oil
2 garlic cloves, peeled
2 teaspoons lemon juice

Gnocchi, but without mashed potatoes? Don't get me wrong, I love a spud, and will shoehorn it into as many recipes as possible, but what if gnocchi could be transformed into a quick, higher-protein dish with no sacrifice to flavor? No precooking of potatoes required, just mash up the beans, add the flour, and away you go.

For the gnocchi, drain the cans of cannellini beans, reserving 3 tablespoons of their liquid. Place the beans in a bowl. Use a fork to mash the beans, then pass them through a sieve or potato ricer to remove any large chunks or skins.

Add the reserved 3 tablespoons bean liquid to the smooth cannellini paste and mix to combine. Add the flour, ¾ teaspoon salt and pepper to taste, and mix until a lumpy, but well-mixed, dough forms. Use your hands to knead until the dough comes together into a ball, for around 2 minutes.

Wrap the dough in plastic wrap and set aside to rest while you make the pesto.

Place a medium saucepan over medium heat. Add the pine nuts and roast until lightly browned. Be careful not to let them burn. Remove from the pan as soon as they're done and transfer to a blender or food processor. Add the remaining ingredients with 1 teaspoon salt and blend until smooth.

Bring a medium saucepan of salted water to a boil.

Unwrap the gnocchi dough and divide in half. Lightly flour a work surface and roll 1 piece of dough into a ½in- (12mm-) wide snake. Slice the roll of dough into ½in (12mm) nuggets and dust with a little flour to keep separated. Repeat with the other half of the dough.

Roll each of the nuggets of dough down the back of a fork to create ridges, then pour them all into the pan of boiling water. Boil until the gnocchi float to the surface. Drain the gnocchi and transfer to a mixing bowl.

Add at least 5 tablespoons of the pesto to the gnocchi and toss to coat. Divide between 2 warmed bowls and serve with a little more vegan Parmesan and some pepper.

Dinner

"Jazz up the dinner table without resorting to cringey ice-breakers like an episode of *Come Dine With Me* (dear Lord, what a sad little life, Jane)."

I get it, you came here for vegan dinners; you probably even flicked your way straight to this chapter before you left the book store. That's because we're all constantly searching for a way to jazz up the dinner table without resorting to cringey ice-breakers like an episode of *Come Dine With Me* (dear Lord, what a sad little life, Jane). I guarantee you came to the right place.

You'll notice I've divided things up into school night dinners (when you're low on time and dangerously hangry) and date night dinners (when you're ready to push that proverbial boat out). As a vegan blogger, I'm often torn between easy breezy recipes and more hands-on dishes. Likewise, I'll bet some of you are here to learn how to feed a pack of ravenous vegans in less than thirty minutes, while others are pumped at the idea of investing all day in the kitchen over a meal for one. The truth is, both kinds of cooking can be joyful if you do them right, and you'll find recipes suited to both in this chapter.

Also, a note on my use of the term "date night." If you think these recipes don't apply to you because you're single and unwilling to mingle, you're dead wrong. Likewise, if you're cooking for a family of five, there's also something for you in this section. To me, "date night" just means "a little bit fancy." It's the night when you get out the posh plates because you've worked hard on this dinner, and even sprinkled chopped parsley on top. Regardless of how many people are sitting at the table, date night dinners are just that little bit extra.

School Night Fettuccine Alfredo

☺ x 2

14oz (400g) can cannellini beans
1 cup (220ml) soy milk
3 tablespoons nutritional yeast
1 tablespoon lemon juice
1 tablespoon tapioca flour
2 tablespoons olive oil
3 tablespoons Vegan Butter (see page 272), or store-bought vegan butter
3 garlic cloves, crushed or finely grated
9oz (250g) vegan fettuccine (not egg pasta!) Handful parsley leaves, torn, to serve (optional)
Sea salt flakes and freshly ground black pepper

Equipment needed
High-speed blender

I'm not sure who the original Alfredo was, but imagine having one of the most comforting pasta experiences known to humankind named after you! He must've been a seriously chill dude. Do your best to channel Alfredo while making this dish; it shouldn't be hard because the recipe's a total breeze. The sauce requires only a blender and is so silky-smooth it hugs the noodles like that ski onesie on Ned Flander's tush.

Bring a large saucepan of water to a boil and salt generously.

Meanwhile, place the cannellini beans and the liquid from the can into a high-speed blender along with the soy milk, nutritional yeast, lemon juice, tapioca flour, and olive oil. Blend until smooth.

Place a frying pan for which you have a lid over medium heat and add the vegan butter. When melted, add the garlic and fry for 2 minutes, making sure it doesn't burn or brown.

Add the cannellini cream and stir well to combine. Season with a pinch of salt and ¼ teaspoon pepper, then reduce the heat to low and cover with the lid.

Add the fettuccine to the boiling salted water and cook until al dente, according to the package instructions. Drain over a bowl, reserving the pasta water.

Add the cooked pasta to the cannellini cream and stir to coat. If the sauce is too thick, loosen it up with a little of the reserved pasta water.

Divide the pasta between warmed bowls and sprinkle with a little extra pepper and/or the torn parsley before serving.

Two Tin Tagine

☺ x 2

2 tablespoons extra-virgin
    olive oil
1 large onion, finely sliced
4 garlic cloves, crushed
2 tablespoons finely chopped
    parsley leaves, their
    stems finely chopped and
    kept separate
2 teaspoons garam masala
¼ teaspoon chili powder
5 dried apricots, chopped
3½oz (100g) flaked almonds,
    plus more (optional)
    toasted flaked almonds,
    to serve
1 cinnamon stick (or
    ¼ teaspoon ground
    cinnamon)
2 tablespoons tomato purée
1 tablespoon harissa paste
1 eggplant, or small butternut
    squash or pumpkin, cut
    into cubes
14oz (400g) can chickpeas,
    drained
14oz (400g) can plum
    tomatoes
17oz (500ml) vegetable stock
Juice 1 lemon
Small bunch mint leaves
½ red onion, finely sliced
1 tablespoon pine nuts
    (optional)
Sea salt and freshly ground
    black pepper

I long to be able to cook like my Mam. As a kid, I'd watch in awe as she rummaged through the cupboards, pulled out a handful of cans, spices, and dry ingredients, then made dinner for five before you knew it. For this recipe, I'm channeling Mam. It isn't exactly quick, but it's easy, hands-off, and requires few specialized ingredients. It calls for an eggplant, but will also work beautifully with butternut squash or pumpkin, depending on which you have.

Place a cast-iron casserole dish for which you have a lid over medium-low heat and add the olive oil. Once the pan is hot, add the onion and fry lightly for 1 minute. Add the garlic and parsley stems and fry for another 2 minutes. Do not allow the onion or garlic to brown.

Add the ground spices, apricots, and almonds and stir well to coat the onion. Snap the cinnamon stick and add to the pot with the tomato purée and harissa. Cook for a few minutes more, stirring, until the tomato purée has darkened and the mixture is highly fragrant.

Add the eggplant, or squash or pumpkin, chickpeas, tomatoes, and stock. Stir well, season to taste, and bring to a simmer.

Cover the pot with the lid and leave to simmer for 40 minutes, stirring occasionally, until thickened, rich, and saucy. Taste and season with salt and pepper accordingly.

Stir in the lemon juice and top with the parsley leaves, mint, red onion, and pine nuts or toasted flaked almonds.

Serve with pita breads, rice, or couscous.

Dinner:
School Night

Level ①②③

Hash Brown Cottage Pie

☺ x 4

22oz (630g) bag frozen
   hash browns
4½oz (125g) fresh shiitake
   mushrooms
3 tablespoons olive oil
1 large onion, finely chopped
1 garlic clove, crushed
1 celery rib, finely chopped
2 carrots, finely chopped
14oz (400g) can green or
   brown lentils, drained
2 tablespoons all-purpose
   flour
1 tablespoon tomato purée
1 teaspoon Dijon mustard
2 teaspoons balsamic
   vinegar
2 teaspoons Marmite
2 tablespoons dark soy sauce
2 bay leaves
½ teaspoon dried thyme
3 cups (700ml) vegetable
   stock
2 teaspoons vegetable oil
3 tablespoons soy milk
Sea salt flakes and freshly
   ground black pepper

Everyone knows the best bit about cottage pie is the golden-brown, crispy bits on top. Everyone also knows that the worst bit about cottage pie is making the mashed potatoes—enough already—just give me that crispy, golden, spud-topped pie pronto! So, in exchange for thirty minutes of your time, I'll give you a recipe that eliminates all the hassle and skips to the good stuff, thanks to hash browns. My fave, frozen, crispy potato shreds work perfectly and cook in minutes, so this recipe is ideal for feeding the fam after a long day.

Preheat the oven to 400°F (200°C) convection. Remove the hash browns from the freezer and leave to defrost while you prepare the pie filling.

Using the largest holes on a box grater, shred the shiitake mushrooms. Transfer to a bowl and set aside.

Heat a large ovenproof saucepan, or cast-iron casserole dish, over medium heat. Add the olive oil and heat. Fry the onion and garlic until soft, then add the shredded shiitakes, celery, carrots, and drained lentils. Fry for 3–5 minutes more, the carrots are softening and the shredded shiitakes are soft.

Add the flour, tomato purée, mustard, balsamic, Marmite, soy sauce, bay leaves, and dried thyme.

Stir to coat everything with the flour, then pour in the vegetable stock. Bring to a boil, stirring occasionally, then reduce the heat and allow to simmer for about 10 minutes.

Taste the sauce: it should be browned and nicely reduced. Season with salt and pepper, then remove from the heat.

In a bowl, break up the defrosted hash browns into shreds. Add the vegetable oil, soy milk, a pinch of salt, and ¼ teaspoon pepper, then mix with your hands.

Top the filling with the shredded hash browns and place in the oven for 20 minutes. Remove from the oven when the top looks crisp and golden brown.

> **Recipe note**
> Here we use a combo of lentils and shiitake mushrooms for a ground beef substitute. If you want an even meatier pie, swap those for 14oz (400g) frozen or refrigerated store-bought vegan ground beef. For a cheap and cheerful option, use 7oz (200g) ground TVP, first rehydrating it in just-boiled water for at least 10 minutes.

**Dinner:
School Night**

Level

Squashio e Pepe

☺ x 2

1 small butternut squash
   14–18oz (400–500g)
   before peeling
¼ cup (60g) Vegan Butter
   (see page 272), or store-
   bought vegan butter
10½oz (300g) vegan pasta
   (not egg pasta!)
7oz (200ml) soy milk
2 tablespoons white miso
   paste
1½ tablespoons nutritional
   yeast
1 tablespoon tapioca flour
½ tablespoon coarsely
   ground black pepper,
   plus more to serve
1 teaspoon sea salt flakes
Grateable Parmesan
   (see page 255), or vegan
   Parmesan, finely grated,
   to serve

Butternut squash deserves some sort of award, if you ask me. Not only does it sound like the Benedict Cumberbatch of the veg patch, but it tastes exactly as its name sounds. When roasted, it's buttery, nutty, and easy to squash, and that's exactly why it works so well in this recipe. The squash blends up incredibly smoothly to make an irresistibly umami sauce, peppered with, well, pepper.

Preheat the oven to 400°F (200°C) convection.

Halve the butternut squash lengthwise and place on a baking sheet cut-side up. Scoop out the seeds and rub half the vegan butter over the orange flesh with ½ tablespoon coarsely ground pepper. Place in the oven to roast for 1 hour, or until fork-soft. Remove from the oven and leave to cool for 5 minutes.

Meanwhile, heat a large pot of salted water over medium heat until boiling and add the pasta.

While the pasta boils, use a spoon to scoop the roasted squash flesh out of its skin (discard the skin). Transfer the squash flesh to a blender and add the remaining vegan butter, the soy milk, miso paste, nutritional yeast, tapioca flour, and 1 teaspoon salt. Blend until very smooth.

Once the pasta is al dente, use a ladle to reserve 1¾ cups (400ml) of the pasta water, then drain the pasta and return it to the empty pan.

Add the blended butternut squash mixture to the cooked pasta along with the reserved cooking water and place over low heat.

Stirring constantly, cook for 1 minute, or until the sauce is just hot. Serve immediately with extra coarsely ground pepper and vegan Parmesan.

Dinner:
School Night

Level

Tempeh Nuggies

Makes 12

¾ cup (100g) cornstarch

7oz (200ml) soy milk

2 teaspoons lemon juice

¾ cup (80g) panko bread crumbs

2 tablespoons vegetable oil

1 teaspoon smoked paprika

Pinch ground turmeric

½ teaspoon garlic powder

¼ teaspoon dried oregano

14oz (400g) tempeh, chopped into 1in (2.5cm) nuggets

Sea salt flakes and freshly ground black pepper

1 quantity Gochujang Barbecue Sauce (see page 265), or ketchup, to serve

What is tempeh and why do I fear it so?

Don't fear tempeh! It's such a useful, delicious, and versatile vegan ingredient. Unlike tofu, which is made from soy milk curds, tempeh is made from whole soybeans, which are packed into a block shape and fermented. Because they're aged in this way, tempeh has considerably more flavor and texture than tofu. You can slice it into strips, break it into nuggets, or crumble it up like a ground meat substitute.

Can I tempeh you to try a nugget? Wait, no, that was rubbish, let me try again. Don't lose your tempeh over how delicious these nuggies are. Scrap that. Get ready to share these nuggies with your contempehraries. Ugh! How are these getting worse? Look, I'm not good at Dad jokes, but I know my nuggies, and these are top tier. Go on, give in to tempehtion.... Oh, I give up!

Preheat the oven to 350°F (180°C) convection and line a baking sheet with parchment paper.

Take 3 bowls. Put the cornstarch in bowl 1. In bowl 2, place the soy milk, add the lemon juice, and whisk well. The milk should thicken quickly. In bowl 3, place, the panko, vegetable oil, spices, and herbs, 1 teaspoon salt, and ¼ teaspoon pepper, stirring well to distribute everything evenly.

Place a nugget of tempeh into the cornstarch. Using one hand, make sure the nugget is completely coated. Tap the nugget on the side of the bowl to remove any excess cornstarch.

Transfer the nugget to the soy-milk mixture. Using the other hand, make sure the nugget is coated. Remove and allow the excess liquid to drip back into the bowl. Place the coated nugget back into the cornstarch.

Using the first hand, coat the nugget in cornstarch again and then back into the soy-milk mixture so that the nugget has 2 layers of cornstarch and 2 layers of soy-milk mixture.

Drop the coated nugget into the bread crumbs and toss the bowl to make sure the nugget is completely coated. Remove from the bread crumbs with a fork and place on the baking sheet.

Repeat the process with the remaining tempeh nuggets until they're all completely coated and arranged on the baking sheet. You can do the coating process 2–3 nuggets at a time, if you're in a rush.

Bake for a total of 35 minutes, flipping after 20 minutes.

Serve hot with Gochujang Barbecue Sauce, ketchup, and your favorite dip.

Dinner:
School Night

Level

Hands-Free Orzo Puttanesca

☺ x 4

2 tablespoons olive oil
1 red onion, finely chopped
3 garlic cloves, crushed or
    finely grated
1 teaspoon nori flakes
2 tablespoons capers, finely
    chopped, plus 2 tablespoon
    whole capers
1 teaspoon dried oregano
1 tablespoon tomato purée
5 sundried tomatoes,
    finely chopped
4½oz (120g) pitted black
    olives, sliced into rings
9oz (250g) orzo
14oz (400g) can chopped
    tomatoes
14oz (400g) can whole
    plum tomatoes
2 cups (450ml) vegetable
    stock
Pinch chili flakes
4 tablespoons Vegan
Mozzarella (see page 252),
    or store-bought vegan
    mozzarella
Leaves from small bunch
    parsley, finely chopped

So, you want a hands-free dinner? Baby, this orzo recipe is the Bluetooth headset of pastas! Once your onion is fried, it's just a case of popping in the remaining ingredients, topping with a lid and baking. Now your hands are free to do all sorts of important activities, such as conducting a séance, entering a competitive yo-yo championship, or pensively stroking a beard (ideally your own). And when you're done, a delicious pan of orzo awaits.

Preheat the oven to 400°F (200°C) convection.

Place a medium ovenproof saucepan over medium heat and add the olive oil. Heat, then add the onion, garlic, nori, and capers. Fry for 2–3 minutes, until the onion is just starting to turn translucent.

Add the remaining ingredients except for the mozzarella and parsley. Bring to a simmer and stir well. Cover with a tight-fitting, ovenproof lid and bake in the oven for 30 minutes.

Take the pot from the oven and remove the lid. Preheat the broiler.

Top the baked orzo with the vegan mozzarella and broiler until golden and bubbling. Sprinkle with the parsley and serve immediately.

Beluga Dal with Quick Kachumber

☺ x 4

1 tablespoon Vegan Butter
(see page 272), or store-
bought vegan butter

½ teaspoon black mustard
seeds

1 small onion, finely chopped

2in (5cm) piece of ginger,
peeled and finely chopped

6 garlic cloves, crushed or
finely grated

½ teaspoon chili powder

1 teaspoon garam masala

¼ cup (65g) tomato purée

2 x 14oz (400g) cans of
beluga lentils, drained

1¾ cups (400ml) water

1 shallot, very finely chopped

¼ cucumber, very finely
chopped

Leaves from small bunch
mint, finely chopped

Leaves from small bunch
cilantro, finely chopped

1 tablespoon lime juice

¼ cup (60ml) coconut cream

When you get in line at the DMV (Department for Managing Vegans) to apply for your vegan card, the first thing they ask you is, "What's your dal recipe?" That's because dal is one of the most fundamental aspects of being a vegan and it's your legal duty to commit a recipe to memory. This is my go-to, which you're welcome to use in any DMV emergency. I use canned beluga lentils because they hold their shape better than most, so the final product still has some bite. If you'd rather use dried lentils like a traditional dal, then go for it! Just be sure to cook them before starting this recipe.

Place a medium saucepan over medium heat and add the vegan butter. Once hot, add the black mustard seeds and fry for about 30 seconds. Add the onion and fry until soft, but do not let it brown.

Add the ginger, garlic, chili powder, garam masala, and tomato purée. Stir well and fry for another 2 minutes. Add the drained lentils along with the water. Bring to a simmer, then allow to simmer for 15 minutes.

While the dal cooks, make your kachumber by combining the shallot, cucumber, mint, cilantro, and lime juice.

Once the dal is nicely reduced and glossy, remove from the heat. Serve in warmed bowls, swirling in the coconut cream and topping with a few tablespoons of kachumber.

Dinner:
School Night

Level ①②③

Dropped-the-Pot Lasagne

☺ x 4–5

You've heard of ugly dog competitions, you've heard of ugly cake competitions, but here's my submission to the ugly lasagne competition! This is truly the lasagne only a mother could love. But, despite looking like it's been dropped from a great height (hence the name), it makes up for it in convenience and DELICIOUSNESS! No layering required and only one pot to wash at the end of the day.

For the creamy sauce
10½oz (300g) carton
    silken tofu
3oz (100ml) soy milk
3 tablespoons nutritional
    yeast
¼ cup (30g) tapioca flour
2 tablespoons vegetable oil
Fine sea salt

For the ragù
2 tablespoons olive oil
1 onion, finely chopped
3 garlic cloves, crushed
9oz (250g) frozen vegan
    ground beef
1 teaspoon dried oregano
2 tablespoons tomato purée
2 tablespoons dark soy
    sauce
2 x 14oz (400g) cans
    chopped tomatoes
1¼ cups (300ml) vegan
    stock
Freshly ground black
    pepper

For the rest
6–8 vegan lasagne sheets
    (not egg lasagne!)
Leaves from small bunch
    basil, finely chopped

Equipment needed
High-speed blender (optional)

Preheat the oven to 350°F (180°C) convection.

Place the creamy sauce ingredients in the bowl of a high-speed blender with ½ teaspoon salt and blend until smooth. Alternatively, place the ingredients in a tall container and blend with an immersion blender until very smooth. Set aside.

For the ragù, set a large ovenproof pan for which you have a lid over medium heat. Add the olive oil and heat. Add the onion and garlic and fry for 2 minutes.

Add the mince, oregano, tomato purée, soy sauce, tomatoes, and stock. Stir and bring to a simmer. Cover with the lid and allow to simmer for 15 minutes, stirring every now and then.

Remove the lid and turn off the heat. Stir three-quarters of the creamy sauce through the ragù. Snap each lasagne sheet into 4 pieces and stir into the ragù. Place in the oven to bake for 30–35 minutes.

Remove from the oven and preheat the broiler.

Top the lasagne with the remaining creamy sauce and place under the broiler until golden and bubbly, around 5 minutes. Top with the basil and serve.

Dinner:
School Night

Level

Butternut Steaks with Chimichurri

☺ x 4

For the steaks
1 large butternut squash
2 teaspoons olive oil
1 tablespoon liquid smoke
1 garlic clove, crushed or
  finely grated

For the chimichurri
1 large bunch cilantro
1 large bunch parsley
3 garlic cloves, peeled
Juice 2 limes
½ cup (120ml) extra-virgin
  olive oil
Sea salt flakes and freshly
  ground black pepper

You know when you deliberately avoid a particular band because your ex used to love them and you've made an unbreakable association? Well, that's exactly what I did with chimichurri, except I avoided it because I associated it with meat. In reality, chimichurri is a delicious salsa that belongs on many vegan plates (especially mine), but particularly on these seared butternut steaks.

Place all the ingredients for the chimichurri in a blender or food processor with 1 teaspoon salt and ½ teaspoon pepper and pulse-blend until you have a chunky salsa.

For the steaks, using a sharp knife, remove the rounded bulb end from the butternut squash and reserve for another recipe.

Take the cylindrical part of the butternut squash, peel it, then slice lengthwise into 4 steaks. Score diamonds on both sides of each piece of butternut.

Heat a large frying pan—or you may need 2 pans—over medium-low heat and add 1 teaspoon of the olive oil. Once hot, add the squash steaks. Cook for 20 minutes, flipping the steaks every few minutes. While the steaks cook, whisk together the remaining olive oil, liquid smoke, and garlic with a pinch more each of salt and pepper.

Once the steaks are just fork-tender, brush with the liquid smoke mixture and fry for another 30–60 seconds on each side, making sure the garlic doesn't burn.

Once the butternut steaks are cooked through and golden brown, drizzle with the chimichurri.

Serve with a side of fries and the remaining chimichurri.

Dinner:
School Night

Level  1 ⟨2⟩ ⟨3⟩

Spaghetti and Borlotti Balls

☺ x 2

For the borlotti balls
14oz (400g) can borlotti beans, drained
3½oz (100g) ground TVP
2 teaspoons vegan beef stock powder
3 tablespoons Bisto gravy granules
2 teaspoons mushroom powder
½ teaspoon onion powder
½ teaspoon garlic powder
1 teaspoon Marmite
3oz (100ml) boiling water

For the pasta
1 quantity Makin Marinara (see page 270), or store-bought vegan tomato sauce
10½oz (300g) vegan spaghetti (not egg pasta!)
Sea salt
Grateable Parmesan (see page 255), or store-bought vegan Parmesan, to serve
Fresh basil, finely chopped, to serve (optional)

Equipment needed
High-speed blender (optional)

Name a more romantic scene than the spaghetti and meatballs bit from *Lady and the Tramp*. You can't, possibly because Tramp is the second most handsome cartoon character of all time, topped only by the animated Robin Hood: such a fox! But enough about those hunks. Get a load of this vegan take on an Italian classic. I make the meatballs from mashed borlotti beans and ground TVP to keep things satisfyingly meaty, then cook them in a batch of marinara sauce. Here, give it a try *nudges the last meatball over to you with the tip of my nose*.

To make the borlotti balls, place the beans in a bowl and mash with a fork. Don't mash them to a paste; keep things nice and chunky.

Place 2oz (60g) of the ground TVP in a high-speed blender or food processor and blend until finely ground. Add the ground and unground TVP to the borlotti beans and stir to combine.

In a measuring cup, place the stock powder, Bisto, mushroom, onion and garlic powders, and Marmite. Add the boiling water and whisk until smooth. Add to the borlotti mixture and stir well. Wet your hands lightly and form the mixture into 16 balls. Set aside.

Place the marinara sauce in a medium saucepan for which you have a lid and place over medium heat. Once simmering, add the borlotti balls and cover with a lid. Leave to simmer for 15 minutes. If you need to stir the sauce, be very careful not to break up the borlotti balls, since they will be rather delicate.

Bring a large pot of salted water to a boil and add the spaghetti. Cook until al dente, according to the package instructions, then drain, reserving 3oz (100ml) of the pasta water, and return the pasta to the empty pan. Carefully stir the pasta water into the marinara sauce and remove from the heat.

Add a few spoonfuls of sauce to the drained spaghetti and toss to combine. Divide the spaghetti between 2 warmed bowls and top with the remaining sauce and borlotti balls.

Serve with Parmesan and basil if you like.

Dinner:
School Night

Level ① ② ☆③

Crispy Burrito Bowl with Tofu Sofritas

☺ x 2

For the burrito bowls
2 large flour tortillas
2 teaspoons vegetable oil
Sea salt flakes and freshly
    ground black pepper

For the sofritas
2 dried ancho chilies,
    seeded and stemmed
1 dried guajillochili, seeded
    and stemmed
3 garlic cloves, chopped
¼ teaspoon ground cumin
¼ teaspoon dried cilantro
½ teaspoon dried oregano
1 teaspoon paprika
1 tablespoon light brown
    sugar
3 tablespoons white wine
    vinegar
¾ cup (180ml) vegetable
    stock
9oz (250g) extra-firm tofu,
    cubed

To serve
1 large tomato, finely
    chopped
½ onion, finely chopped
small bunch cilantro,
    finely chopped
2¾ cups (500g) cooked rice
1 avocado, peeled, pitted,
    and sliced or cubed
Small bunch cilantro,
    coarsely torn
2 lime wedges

I've got a really embarrassing crush on the tofu sofritas from restaurant chain Chipotle. I know it's fast food, but something about that crumbly tofu in the rich adobo sauce makes my tippy-toes lift off the ground like a loved-up Looney Tune. Never tried it? Here's your chance. I've also put mine in a super-crispy, golden, flour tortilla bowl that took just minutes to make. Hubba, hubba!

To make the burrito bowls, preheat the oven to 350°F (150°C) convection.

Brush each tortilla with the vegetable oil and gently push each one inside a separate medium metal bowl or ovenproof metal colander so the edges of the tortilla become fluted and it creates a bowl shape. (If you've only got one, you'll need to crisp these up one at a time.) Sprinkle each with salt.

Place the bowls or colanders on a baking sheet and bake for 7 minutes. Remove the bowls and flip the tortillas upside down so their unbaked bottoms are exposed. Return to the oven for another 5 minutes, or until golden brown. Remove from the oven and allow to cool fully on a wire rack.

For the sofritas, heat a large frying pan over medium heat. When it is hot, add the chilies and toast them for 30 seconds. Remove the chilies from the pan and place in a bowl. Cover with just-boiled water and leave to hydrate for 10 minutes.

Drain the chilies and place in a blender with all the remaining sofritas ingredients except the extra-firm tofu, adding ½ teaspoon salt and ¼ teaspoon pepper. Blend until you have a smooth sauce.

Return the large frying pan to medium heat and add the cubes of tofu. Cook briefly, until lightly browned. Add the blended sauce and stir to coat. Reduce the heat to simmer and allow to cook for 10–15 minutes, until the sauce is thick and reduced.

Meanwhile, mix the tomato, onion, and cilantro in a small bowl.

Fill the crispy tortilla bowls with a layer of cooked rice topped with the tofu sofritas, tomato mixture, avocado, and cilantro. Squeeze the lime over the top and enjoy.

**Dinner:
School Night**

Level ① ② ③

One Pot Ragù Rigatoni

☺ x 2

1oz (30g) dried shiitake mushrooms
1 tablespoon olive oil
1 onion, finely chopped
4 garlic cloves, crushed or finely grated
1 celery rib, finely chopped
14oz (400g) can green lentils, drained
2 tablespoons brown rice miso paste or red miso paste
¼ cup (60ml) vegan red wine
2 x 14oz (400g) cans chopped tomatoes
1½ cups (350ml) vegetable stock
9oz (250g) vegan rigatoni (not egg pasta!)
2oz (50g) Grateable Parmesan (see page 255), or store-bought vegan Parmesan, to serve
Handful parsley leaves, to serve

Much like for a rapper, timing is key to any successful one-pot pasta dish. Actually, perhaps there are other skills to being a successful rapper that can't be connected to pasta, but allow me some poetic license here. This ragù rigatoni sort of happens before your very eyes like a tomato-based miracle and it's incredibly low maintenance, which makes it perfect if you're entertaining. You know what else is entertaining? RAP MUSIC. Boom! Full circle!

Rehydrate the mushrooms by placing them in a bowl and covering with just-boiled water, then cover and set aside for at least 15 minutes. Once rehydrated, carefully squeeze any excess moisture from the mushrooms back into the bowl and chop them very finely. Reserve the mushroom water.

Place a large saucepan for which you have a lid over medium heat and add the olive oil. When hot, add the onion and fry for 1 minute, or until softening. Add the garlic and fry for 1 minute more.

Add the celery, mushrooms, and drained lentils. Fry everything for another minute, stirring constantly. Add the miso paste, red wine, and tomatoes, then cover and let simmer for 10 minutes, stirring occasionally.

Stir the sauce and add the vegetable stock and rigatoni. Stir to combine. Cover again and reduce the heat to low simmer.

Leave to cook for 10–15 minutes, stirring halfway through. If the sauce looks a little dry, add a little extra boiling water to stop it from sticking.

Remove the lid, stir again, and serve with grated vegan Parmesan and a sprinkle of parsley.

Dinner:
School Night

Level  ① ② ③

Cannellini Mushroom Stroganoff

☺ x 4

14oz (400g) can cannellini beans
2 tablespoons lemon juice
½ cup (120ml) soy milk
3 tablespoons olive oil
21oz (600g) mixed mushrooms, chopped in large chunks
1 onion, chopped
2 garlic cloves, crushed or finely grated
Leaves of 4 thyme sprigs, plus more to serve
1 teaspoon English mustard
1 tablespoon paprika
1 tablespoon all-purpose flour
2 cups (500ml) vegetable stock
Leaves from small bunch parsley
Sea salt and freshly ground black pepper

To serve
Steamed brown rice
Lemon wedges

Equipment needed
High-speed blender

At home, this is what we call a "hug supper," because it's a supper that feels like a hug. Duh. I'll bet there are literally dozens of people ready to cyberbully me off the face of the Earth for serving a strog with brown rice, but don't knock it until you've tried it. In my opinion, it has to be brown rice, for that wholesome nuttiness, and always with a generous squeeze of lemon juice to perk things up.

Place the can of cannellini beans, along with its liquid, the lemon juice, and soy milk in the bowl of a high-speed blender. Blend on high speed until completely smooth. Set aside.

Place a large frying pan over medium heat and add 1 tablespoon of the olive oil. When hot, add the mushrooms and fry until lightly browned on all sides, around 5 minutes. Season with salt and pepper, then remove from the pan and set aside.

Return the pan to the heat and add the remaining 2 tablespoons olive oil. Add the onion and fry until they turn soft. Add the garlic, thyme, mustard, and paprika and fry for 1 minute more. Now stir in the flour, then gradually pour in the stock, stirring continuously.

Bring to a gentle boil, then reduce the heat to low and let simmer for 15–20 minutes, stirring often, until the mixture is reduced by half.

Add the blended cannellini mixture and bring to a simmer, but do not let it boil. Add the cooked mushrooms and parsley, then stir to combine before removing from the heat.

Season with salt and pepper, sprinkle with thyme, and serve with brown rice and lemon wedges to squeeze over before eating.

Dinner:
School Night

Level  ① ② ③

Zha Jiang Mian

 x 2

1½oz (40g) fresh shiitake mushrooms, finely chopped

14oz (400g) can beluga lentils, drained

2 tablespoons soy sauce

2 tablespoons vegetable oil

4 garlic cloves, crushed or finely grated

2in (5cm) piece ginger peeled and finely grated

2 teaspoons cornstarch

9oz (250ml) water

3 tablespoons sweet bean sauce (see recipe note, right)

4 tablespoons ground bean sauce (see recipe note, right)

9½oz (270g) vegan wheat noodles (not egg noodles!)

2 scallions, julienned

2in (5cm) wedge cucumber, julienned

1 carrot, julienned

1 tablespoon Chinese crispy chili oil (Lao Gan Ma), to serve

I cook zha jiang mian all the time. People say this a lot when writing cookbooks to cover up their embarrassment about how often they eat six potato waffles for dinner. Not me though. I have no reason to lie, since the only person likely to buy this book is my Mam, and she already thinks I'm really interesting. Hi, Mam! Anyway, this is my vegan take on the classic Chinese "fried sauce noodles," which are super-popular in Beijing. Traditionally made with minced pork or beef, my quick substitute involves a blend of finely chopped shiitake mushrooms and a can of beluga lentils. Meaty, umami, slurpy goodness that's way better than potato waffles.

In a bowl, combine the chopped shiitake mushrooms, beluga lentils, and soy sauce. Mash gently with a fork to break up the lentils, but do not mash to a paste. Set aside.

Heat a wok for which you have a lid over medium heat and add the vegetable oil. When hot, add the garlic and ginger. Fry for a minute until fragrant, but do not let the garlic burn.

Add the mushroom-lentil mixture and fry for 3 minutes more. If the mix begins to stick to the wok, add a small splash of water to loosen things up.

Meanwhile, in a small bowl, whisk together the cornstarch and water until smooth. Add the sweet bean sauce and ground bean sauce and whisk again. Add this mixture to the wok and reduce the heat to medium-low. Cover with the lid and simmer for 5–8 minutes, stirring occasionally.

Meanwhile, cook the noodles according to the package instructions (some require simmering in a pan and some just need a dunk in boiling water, so be sure to double-check).

Drain the noodles and add to the sauce. Toss to combine and serve topped with the scallions, cucumber, carrot, and crispy chili oil.

Recipe note
If your local supermarket doesn't stock sweet bean and ground bean sauces, your local Asian market will. My favorite brand is Shinho, which comes in a little tub with a yellow clipped lid.

Chicken Parmesan Tenders

☺ x 6

For the chicken

4 fillets Seitan Chicken
    (see page 235)
⅞ cup (100g) all-purpose
    flour
3 tablespoons gram flour
1¼ cups (300ml) soy milk
3 tablespoons lemon juice
3 tablespoons vegetable oil,
    plus more for frying
1½ cups (150g) panko
    bread crumbs
2oz (60g) Grateable
    Parmesan (see page
    255), or store-bought
    vegan Parmesan,
    finely grated
Fine sea salt and freshly
    ground black pepper

For the rest

1 quantity Makin Marinara
    (see page 270), or
    store-bought vegan
    tomato sauce
1 quantity Vegan Mozzarella
    (see page 252),
    or around 7oz (200g)
    store-bought vegan
    melting cheese
5½oz (150g) Grateable
    Parmesan (see page 255),
    or store-bought vegan
    Parmesan, finely grated,
    plus more to serve

To serve

Cooked vegan spaghetti
    (not egg pasta!)
Basil leaves

Show me one part of this meal that doesn't make you feel like you're being hugged by a great big lovely grandma. I'm talking crispy, breaded-chicken tenders on marinara sauce with all the vegan mozzarella and Parmesan you can muster up! In fact, if I were your grandma, I'd be serving you seconds right now and sending you home with a box of leftovers, for the road. Now come give Nana a smooch!

Pull the seitan chicken into roughly 25 tenders in total.

Place the all-purpose flour in a bowl. Dunk the tenders in one at a time to coat all sides, then transfer to a platter.

In a clean bowl, whisk together the gram flour, soy milk, lemon juice, and vegetable oil. In a separate bowl, mix together the panko, Parmesan, ½ teaspoon salt, and ¼ teaspoon pepper.

Working with one tender at a time, dunk it in the soy milk batter, then directly into the panko, making sure it's evenly coated. Return the coated tender to the platter and repeat to coat the rest.

Place a large frying pan over medium heat and add around ½in (1cm) vegetable oil. When hot, lift a tender and carefully place in the oil. Fry a small batch of tenders—so as not to overcrowd the pan—until golden brown on the undersides before flipping and frying the other sides, around 5 minutes total. Remove from the pan and place on a baking sheet lined with paper towels. Repeat to cook the remaining tenders.

Preheat the broiler. Spread three-quarters of the marinara sauce over a 13 x 9in (32 x 23cm) roasting pan casserole dish. Top with the fried chicken tenders, then dot the remaining marinara over the top.

Top with the vegan mozzarella and vegan Parmesan, then place under the broiler until bubbly, melted, and golden brown on top.

Serve on spaghetti and sprinkle with basil and more Parmesan.

Dinner:
School Night

Level ① ② ☆③

Quick Kofta Flatbreads

Makes 4

For the kofta

15oz (430g) soft vegan
    ground beef (See recipe
    note, below right)
½ onion, finely chopped
¼ cup (15g) finely chopped
    parsley leaves
¼ cup (15g) finely chopped
    cilantro
2 tablespoons finely chopped
    mint leaves
1 teaspoon paprika
2 teaspoons garam masala
1 tablespoon harissa paste
⅓ cup (50g) currants or
    raisins
Olive oil, for grilling
Sea salt and freshly ground
    black pepper

To serve

4 flatbreads or pitas
Zankou Garlic Whip (see
    page 266), or store-
    bought vegan mayo
½ cucumber, coarsely
    chopped
Handful cherry tomatoes,
    coarsely chopped
Leaves from small bunch
    parsley, finely chopped
1 red onion, finely chopped
Handful shredded
    cabbage
2 teaspoons pomegranate
    molasses
½ lemon
1 red chili, sliced (optional)

Aaaa! I've gone temporarily dizzy from all the brand-new vegan meat options I just witnessed at my local supermarket. The choice of what to cook is suddenly staggering: call an ambulance! While I'm waiting for it to arrive, I've thought of something fun to do with this package of vegan ground beef I appear to be clutching. How about shaping it into dinky little koftas, packed full of herbs and spices, which makes them ideal for stuffing into flatbreads or pitas? Cancel that ambulance. I'm suddenly feeling much better.

To make the kofta, in a bowl, use your hands to combine all the ingredients, except the olive oil, and season well with salt and pepper. Squeeze the vegan ground beef through your fingers to make sure it has completely broken apart and the herbs and spices are evenly distributed.

Form the kofta into small sausages with tapered ends and thread a skewer through the center of each (or stack 2 on each skewer, if necessary).

Preheat the broiler. Brush the kofta with a little olive oil and place on a baking sheet under the broiler for about 10 minutes, turning occasionally to make sure all sides are browned. Remove from under the broiler.

Gently warm the flatbreads under the broiler, but don't let them brown or crisp up. Top each flatbread with a generous spoonful of garlic whip, the cucumber, tomatoes, parsley, red onion, and cabbage.

Top the flatbreads with the kofta, then drizzle with the pomegranate molasses and a squeeze of lemon juice before serving with the sliced chili on the side, if you like.

> ### Recipe note
> For this recipe, use the vegan ground beef that comes refrigerated and resembles a block of ground beef. This works best here (rather than frozen or dried vegan ground beef) because it holds together and firms up when cooked, so you get a much more satisfyingly meaty bite to the final dish. If you can't find any ground meat like this, you can use vegan burgers instead; they're made from the same stuff!

**Dinner:
School Night**

Level

Sriracha Cashew Chicken

☺ x 4

For the sauce

2 teaspoons mushroom
   bouillon powder

2 tablespoons Shaoxing
   wine (or any Chinese
   cooking wine)

2 teaspoons soy sauce

1½ tablespoons cornstarch

1 teaspoon toasted
   sesame oil

5oz (140ml) water

2 tablespoons sriracha

1 tablespoon sugar

For the stir-fry

14oz (400g) Seitan Chicken
   (see page 235), or 18oz
   (500g) oyster mushrooms

⅔ cup (65g) raw unsalted
   cashews

2 tablespoons vegetable oil

3 garlic cloves, crushed or
   finely grated

Thumb-size piece of
   ginger, peeled and cut
   into matchsticks

1 green bell pepper, sliced
   into strips

2 scallions, sliced
   into strips

1 red chili, finely sliced

Toasted white-sesame
   seeds, to serve

If you have any uncertainty about what a badass my Seitan Chicken is, just wait and see how it soaks up this sriracha sauce *blasts out a sick lick on an electric guitar*. Fling in a few toasted cashews in a devil-may-care manner, chuck in some veggies for crunch, and you're a rock star, baby. Now you can defiantly shove all those junk mail takeout menus in the recycling bin and be sure to put them out on the correct day to ensure they don't go into a landfill... yeahhh, punk rock!

Place all the sauce ingredients in a clean jar and screw on the lid. Shake well until combined, then set aside. The sauce will separate while it sits, so be sure to shake it again before adding to the wok later.

To make the stir-fry, slice the seitan chicken or oyster mushrooms into 1in (2.5cm) chunks. Set aside.

Heat a dry wok or large frying pan over medium heat. Add the cashews and toast for a minute or so, tossing around in the pan regularly to make sure they don't burn. When lightly browned and fragrant, remove from the pan and set aside.

With the wok or pan still over medium heat, add the vegetable oil and heat. Add the garlic and ginger and fry for 1–2 minutes. Do not allow the garlic to burn.

Add the seitan chicken or oyster mushrooms and stir to coat in the oil. Fry for 5 minutes, or until lightly browned. You may need to add a few tablespoons of water to prevent sticking.

Add the green bell pepper and stir-fry for another 2 minutes. Add the scallions and red chili and stir-fry for 1 minute more.

Add the toasted cashews, followed by the sauce (don't forget to shake it up again before adding). Stir well to coat everything with the sauce and immediately reduce the heat to low. The sauce should thicken quickly.

Sprinkle the stir-fry with toasted white-sesame seeds. Serve with steamed rice.

Dinner:
School Night

Level  ① ② ☼

One Pot Shiitake Ramen

☺ × 2

For the broth

1 teaspoon vegetable oil

2 shallots, coarsely chopped

3 garlic cloves, crushed
with a knife

1in (2.5cm) piece ginger,
peeled and sliced

5 dried shiitake mushrooms

2in (5cm) square piece
kombu

4 cups (1 liter) mushroom or
vegetable stock

3 tablespoons brown rice
miso paste

1 tablespoon light tahini

1 teaspoon doubanjiang
(spicy bean paste)

For the ramen

¾lb (350g) assorted fresh
mushrooms, sliced

7oz (200g) ramen noodles
(not egg noodles!)

Greens of 4 scallions,
finely chopped

1 teaspoon toasted
white-sesame seeds

4 vegan boiled egg halves
(see page 86, optional)

Crispy chili oil (Lao Gan Ma),
to serve

Soy sauce, to serve

You might be surprised to hear that I, your fearless cooking companion and spiritual mentor, get intimidated in the kitchen sometimes, but it's true. I'm spooked by many things, including dropping things into a deep-fat fryer, oversized gherkins, and making ramen from scratch. With ramen, it seems like there are just so many elements to get right at the same time, and, yet, I adore eating it. So, consider this my attempt to make a slightly less spooky version, perhaps as exposure therapy. It's all made in the same pot, and it's minimal on ingredients (for a ramen recipe at least), so you can breathe a little sigh of relief.

For the broth, place a large saucepan over medium heat and add the vegetable oil. When hot, add the shallots, garlic, and ginger. Fry for 2 minutes, but do not allow to brown.

Add the mushrooms, kombu, and stock, cover, then bring to a boil. As soon as the broth begins to simmer, remove the kombu. Cover again and reduce the heat slightly. Leave to simmer for 20 minutes.

Pass the broth through a fine-meshed sieve and return it to the pan. Remove the shiitake mushrooms, chop finely, then return them to the pan.

In a bowl, whisk together the miso paste, tahini, and doubanjiang with about ½ cup (120ml) of the broth, then stir this back into the remaining broth on the stove. Reduce the heat to low and cover.

To make the ramen, add the assorted fresh mushrooms to the broth and simmer to cook until softened, about 5 minutes.

Add the ramen noodles and simmer until just cooked, about 3 minutes.

Divide the ramen between 2 warmed bowls, top with the finely chopped scallions and the sesame seeds before serving, with boiled egg halves, if you like. Serve with crispy chili oil and soy sauce.

Dinner:
Date Night

Level ① ② ⟨3⟩

Fancy Fried Chicken

☺ x 2

4 Seitan Chicken fillets (see page 235), or a 14oz (400g) cluster of large oyster mushrooms
½ cup (120g) vegan yogurt
½ cup (120ml) soy milk
2½ cups (300g) all-purpose flour
3 tablespoons cornstarch
2 teaspoons Old Bay seasoning
Vegetable oil, for deep-frying
Fine sea salt and freshly ground black pepper
Your favorite Quick Sauces (see pages 260–270), to serve

Equipment needed
Meat thermometer

It must be Fry-day night, because things are starting to look seriously golden and crispy up in this joint! It doesn't matter if you use homemade seitan or oyster mushrooms, this recipe is all about the crispy coating. Serve it with fries, serve it with buffalo sauce, serve it in a big ol' bucket if you must… whatever gets you in the mood!

Break the seitan chicken into wing-size pieces. If using oyster mushrooms, break the cluster apart into individual mushrooms. Set aside.

In a bowl, whisk together the vegan yogurt and soy milk. In a separate bowl, whisk together the remaining dry ingredients with 2 teaspoons salt and ½ teaspoon pepper.

Pour 3in (7.5cm) vegetable oil into a heavy-bottomed saucepan. Place over medium heat and insert the thermometer to check the temperature. When the oil reaches 350°F (180°C), reduce the heat slightly. Alternatively, fill and heat a deep-fat fryer to 350°F (180°C).

Take 3 pieces of seitan chicken or oyster mushrooms and dredge them thoroughly in the flour mixture using your left hand. Using your right hand, transfer them to the yogurt mixture and make sure they're fully coated. Transfer them once again to the flour mixture and coat them well using your left hand.

Carefully place them in the oil: they should bubble immediately upon contact. Fry the pieces for 8–10 minutes on each side, or until golden brown and crispy. Use a slotted spoon to remove the fried chicken or mushrooms from the oil and place on a baking sheet lined with 2 layers of paper towels.

Repeat the process with the remaining seitan or mushrooms, making sure the oil temperature stays at 350°F (180°C).

Drain and serve with your favorite dipping sauce.

Dinner:
Date Night

Level ① ② ③

Chorizo Bean Stew

😊 x 2

1 teaspoon vegetable oil

10½oz (300g) Seitan
  Chorizo (see page 240),
  or store-bought vegan
  chorizo, sliced into
  thick coins

14oz (400g) can chopped
  tomatoes

2⅓ cups (550ml) vegetable
  stock

14oz (400g) can cannellini,
  butter, or borlotti
  beans, drained

Small bunch parsley,
  coarsely chopped

⅔ cup (150ml) extra-virgin
  olive oil

Sea salt and freshly ground
  black pepper

What's that noise? *BASH!* Your door blasts off its hinges and spins dangerously across the room as sunlight streams through the gaping frame! It's the particularly aggressive arrival of the British summer *children scream in confusion!* and it wants you to know it could disappear at any moment! Quick! Go and spread your body over the largest surface area possible—this could be your last chance to absorb vitamin D for months! Don't wait for me, just go; my job here is to make us a dinner that tastes like we're anywhere, anywhere but England... and I think I have just the recipe.

Place a medium saucepan for which you have a lid over medium heat. Once hot, add vegetable oil and vegan chorizo. Fry for a minute, or until lightly browned on both sides. Remove half the chorizo from the pan and set aside.

Add the can of tomatoes, the stock, and drained beans to the remaining chorizo in the saucepan and bring to a simmer. Cover with a lid and let simmer for 20–25 minutes, stirring occasionally.

While the stew simmers, place the parsley stems and leaves in a blender and add the olive oil. Pulse-blend a few times until the oil is bright green and the parsley is finely chopped.

Season the stew with salt and pepper. Top with the reserved chorizo and a drizzle of the parsley oil.

Dinner:
Date Night

Level ① ② ⟨3⟩

Dinner:
Date Night

Level ① ② ☆3☆

Beefless Bourguignon

☺ x 4

3 tablespoons olive oil

14oz (400g) Seitan Chunks (see page 243), or store-bought vegan chunks, or fresh, peeled beets, chopped into ¾in (2cm) pieces

1 large onion, coarsely chopped

5 garlic cloves, crushed or finely grated

1 large carrot, chopped into ½in (1cm) semicircles

2 tablespoons tomato purée

3 tablespoons all-purpose flour

1½ cups (350ml) vegan red wine (Pinot Noir works great)

1¼ cups (300ml) vegan stock

2 cups (475ml) boiling water

4–5 parsley stalks

4 thyme sprigs

3 rosemary sprigs

3 bay leaves

6 pearl onions or shallots, halved

7oz (200g) mushrooms, chopped into large chunks

2 tablespoons coarsely chopped parsley leaves

Sea salt flakes and freshly ground black pepper

We all need to feel a little bougie sometimes and nothing screams rustic understated class like this French dream dish. What a fantasy to sit down and indulge in the rich luxury of this glossy umami-fest, knowing it's completely plant-based! I'm obsessed with the way the sauce transforms once cooked and how it glazes the chunky seitan and vegetables. Wooh! It's all getting a bit steamy!

Preheat the oven to 350°F (180°C) convection.

Place a large, ovenproof saucepan or cast-iron casserole dish over medium heat and add 1 tablespoon olive oil. When hot, drop in the seitan chunks and fry for about 3 minutes, stirring occasionally until lightly browned. Remove the seitan chunks from the pan and set aside on a plate. If using beets, skip this step.

Add another 1 tablespoon olive oil to the pan, followed by the onion. Fry for a minute, but don't let it brown. Add the garlic and fry for 1 minute more before adding the carrot. Fry for another 3 minutes. If the onion or garlic start to stick, add a small splash of water.

Season with a pinch of salt and ½ teaspoon pepper, then stir in the tomato purée and flour. Pour in half the wine and stir well to make sure no lumps of flour remain. Add the rest of the wine, the stock, and boiling water. Bring to a simmer, then add the seitan chunks or beet chunks.

Gather the parsley stems, thyme, rosemary, and bay in a little muslin or cheesecloth and tie with chef's

twine to make a bouquet garni. Add to the stew. Cover with a lid and place in the oven for 40 minutes.

When the stew is nearly done, place a medium frying pan over medium heat and add the remaining 1 tablespoon oil. Fry the pearl onions or shallots until nicely browned (about 2 minutes) and then add the mushrooms. Fry for a few minutes more, until the mushrooms are cooked and juicy. Season with salt and pepper.

Remove the stew from the oven and remove the lid. Add the fried shallots and mushrooms. Stir to combine, then top with the parsley. Remove the bouquet garni and serve right away with mashed potatoes, or simply as is.

> **Recipe note**
> Obviously, this recipe works best with my vegan Seitan Chunks, but if you're short on time don't worry. You can either use store-bought vegan chunks or opt for a "beet bourguignon" instead and substitute fresh, peeled beets. You'll get a beautiful chestnut-red sauce with a wonderful earthy twist.

Dinner:
Date Night

Level ① ② ③

Cowboy Beans with Cornbread Dumplings

🙂 x 4

For the beans

3 king oyster mushrooms
3 tablespoons vegetable oil
1 onion, finely chopped
3 garlic cloves, crushed or finely grated
½ teaspoon smoked paprika
½ teaspoon ground cumin
½ teaspoon ground cilantro
¼ teaspoon cayenne pepper
1½ tablespoons dark soy sauce
2 teaspoons chipotle paste
9oz (250ml) just-boiled water
¼ cup (60ml) ketchup
2 tablespoons liquid smoke
14oz (400g) can chopped tomatoes, drained
2 x 14oz (400g) cans pinto beans, or red kidney beans, drained
2 tablespoons vegan bouillon powder
2 tablespoons bourbon whiskey (optional)
1 tablespoon maple syrup
Sea salt flakes and freshly ground black pepper

For the dumplings

⅞ cup (100g) all-purpose flour
⅔ cup (100g) coarse cornmeal or polenta
2 tablespoons sugar
½ tablespoon baking powder
5 tablespoons (70g) Vegan Butter (see page 272), or store-bought vegan butter, melted
⅓ cup (80ml) soy milk
½ teaspoon rice vinegar

To serve (optional)

Sliced green chilies
Grated vegan cheese

Name a better duo than beans and cornbread... you can't! It's impossible. That's why I'm such a fan of this recipe where the two are combined into one dish. The dumplings are scooped onto the umami-rich beans, then they're all whacked in the oven to cook together. It's the ultimate one-pot wonder. Who knew cowboys were so eager to avoid doing dishes?

Preheat the oven to 400°F (200°C) convection.

Use 2 forks to coarsely shred the mushrooms. Set aside.

Place a medium ovenproof saucepan or cast-iron casserole dish for which you have a lid over medium heat and add the vegetable oil. When hot, add the onion and garlic and fry for a few minutes until the onion is starting to turn translucent, but don't let the garlic burn.

Add the spices and shredded mushrooms and fry together for a couple of minutes, or until the mushrooms are soft. Add the soy sauce and chipotle paste and stir. Cook for a few minutes more to temper the spices, adding a splash of water if necessary.

Add the remaining ingredients with ½ teaspoon salt and ¼ teaspoon pepper and stir gently to combine. Bring to a simmer, then cover with the lid and leave to cook for about 10 minutes.

Meanwhile, make the dumplings. In a large bowl, combine the flour, cornmeal, sugar, and baking powder with ½ teaspoon salt. Whisk well to combine.

In a small bowl, combine the melted vegan butter, soy milk, and the rice vinegar. Add to the flour mixture and very briefly whisk to form a coarse batter, but don't overwork it.

Remove the lid from the beans and spoon tablespoon-size blobs of cornbread batter on top. Cover with the lid again and place in the preheated oven to bake for 20 minutes.

Remove the lid and bake for 5 minutes more, or until the dumplings are puffed up and lightly browned.

Remove from the oven and serve with sliced chilies and cheese, if you like.

Dinner:
Date Night

Level ① ② ⑳

Fish Supper

 x 2

For the fish
1 large eggplant
1 large sheet nori seaweed
1 cup (100g) all-purpose
    flour

For the perfect chips
1¼ lb (550g) potatoes
    (Russets work best),
    peeled and sliced into
    ½–¾ in- (1–2cm-) wide
    chips (french fries)
3 tablespoons malt vinegar,
    plus more to serve
Sea salt flakes

➡

"Chips, curry, and a separate barm please!" That's been my order at the chippy shop since I was old enough to talk. Now I live on the south coast of England and even though the word "barm" is utterly meaningless down here (it's just a bread roll, folks, nothing fancy), my love for a chippy supper remains strong. Here's my dream fish supper, made using eggplant wrapped in a crispy nori skin.

To prepare the fish, fill a medium pan halfway with boiling water and place over medium heat. Top with a steamer basket.

Prick the eggplant all over with a fork and slice off the top stem. Place in the steamer to cook for 20 minutes, rotating halfway. Remove the eggplant from the steamer and leave to cool for a few minutes to make it easier to handle.

Slice the eggplant in half lengthwise. Very carefully, use a spoon to scoop out the inside flesh, doing your best to keep the spoon as close to the skin as possible and making sure the flesh all stays in 2 "fillets."

Slice the nori sheet in half and lay on a clean work surface. Top a nori half-sheet with a fillet of eggplant and press down gently so the sheet sticks. Trim off any excess nori and reserve the trimmings for making nori flakes for other recipes. Repeat with the remaining eggplant fillet and nori.

Place the flour in a baking pan and shake to distribute into an even layer. Dunk the eggplant fillets in the flour on all sides to coat, then set aside.

To blanch the chips (fries), place the cut potatoes in a large bowl and just cover with cold water. Add the malt vinegar and 1 teaspoon salt and swirl everything around with your hands. Set the bowl aside for at least 20 minutes, or ideally overnight.

When you're ready to cook, drain the potatoes and dry thoroughly with a clean dish towel.

Dinner:
Date Night

Level ① ②

Fish Supper

To fry and serve
Vegetable oil, for deep-frying
1¾ cups (200g) flour
1½ teaspoons baking powder
3 tablespoons cornstarch
10½oz (275ml) chilled
    vegan beer
14oz (400g) can mushy peas

Equipment needed
Meat thermometer

Fill a large saucepan or deep-fat fryer with 3–4in (8–10cm) vegetable oil and place over medium heat.

Test the oil temperature with the thermometer. When it reaches 280°F (140°C), gently lower half the chips into the oil. Fry for 5–8 minutes, keeping an eye on the oil temperature. Remove the chips with a slotted spoon when they have softened, but before they're browned, to a baking sheet lined with paper towels. Repeat with the other half of the chips.

In a large bowl, mix together the flour, baking powder, and cornstarch. Add the beer and stir together gently with a fork or 2 chopsticks, but do not whisk or overwork the batter.

Increase the temperature of the oil to 350°F (180°C). Transfer the can of mushy peas to a small saucepan and place over low heat to warm through.

Dunk 1 of the floured eggplant fillets into the batter, then carefully lower it into the oil. Immediately also lower half the blanched chips into the oil and fry together for 5 minutes, or until everything is golden brown and crispy.

Remove from the oil and drain on a baking sheet lined with paper towels. Repeat with the remaining eggplant fillet and chips.

Serve with a sprinkle of salt, malt vinegar, and the mushy peas on the side.

Dinner:
Date Night

Level ①②

Smoky Squash Arancini

Photographed on page 151

Makes 8–10

For the risotto

10½oz (300g) peeled butternut squash

2 tablespoons vegan bouillon powder

½ tablespoon olive oil

½ onion, finely chopped

2 garlic cloves, crushed or finely grated

1 teaspoon smoked paprika

½ teaspoon finely chopped sage leaves

1¼ cups (250g) arborio rice

¼ cup (60ml) vegan white wine

2 tablespoons Vegan Butter (see page 272), or store-bought vegan butter

Sea salt and freshly ground black pepper

To coat and fry

1 cup (100g) all-purpose flour

3 tablespoons gram flour

⅔ cup (150ml) any plant milk

1 cup (100g) bread crumbs

Vegetable oil, for deep-frying

Aah, arancini! The Italian word that translates to "little oranges." Of course, they're not actually deep-fried oranges, that would be a really unpleasant and probably highly explosive experience. They're risotto balls! In this case, they're made with a slightly smoky butternut squash risotto, coated in golden bread crumbs. Make them as big or as small as you like, just please don't deep-fry an orange or I'll have to tell Mom.

To make the risotto, peel and halve the squash. Remove the seeds. Slice one half of the squash into ¼in (5mm) cubes. Coarsely grate the other half. Set aside.

Fill a large saucepan with 6 cups (1.5 liters) boiling and place over low heat. Whisk in the bouillon powder.

Place a separate medium saucepan over medium heat and add the olive oil. When hot, add the onion and fry for 1 minute. Now add the garlic and fry for 1 minute more, but do not let the garlic brown. Add the smoked paprika and sage and stir.

Add the arborio rice and stir to coat. Leave the rice to toast for around 30 seconds before adding the white wine. Stir to combine.

Add the grated and cubed squash and stir. Use a ladle to spoon some of the stock from the other saucepan into the risotto, so the rice is just covered. Cook until

the liquid is all absorbed before adding another ladle of stock. Repeat until all the stock is used up before seasoning with salt and pepper, if necessary. Once cooked, remove from the heat and stir in the vegan butter.

Spread the risotto out on a baking sheet to allow it to cool for at least 1 hour before transferring to the fridge for at least another hour, or ideally overnight.

To coat the arancini, in a bowl, whisk together the flours and plant milk to make a batter. In another bowl, place the bread crumbs and ¼ teaspoon salt.

Dampen your hands and form the chilled risotto into 8–10 balls.

Dinner: Date Night

Level ① ② ③

Smoky Squash Arancini

To serve (optional)
1 quantity Makin Marinara
  (see page 270), or
  store-bought vegan
  tomato sauce
Handful Grateable
  Parmesan (see page
  255), or store-bought
  vegan Parmesan,
  finely grated
Handful basil leaves,
  shredded

Equipment needed
Meat thermometer

Very gently, roll a rice ball first in the batter, then in the bread crumbs. Set gently on a baking sheet. Repeat this process until all the rice balls are coated.

Place a medium saucepan over medium-low heat and add 2–3in (5–7.5cm) vegetable oil. Using a meat or candy thermometer to measure the temperature, bring the oil to 340°F (170°C). If you don't have a thermometer, drop a small square of bread into the oil: if it bubbles right away and browns gently, then you're at the correct temperature.

Reduce the heat to low and, using a slotted spoon, lower an arancini into the oil. It should bubble immediately (if not, your oil is too cold) and should brown in around 2 minutes on each side. Fry in small batches, so as not to overcrowd the pan.

Remove the arancini once cooked and place on a few sheets of paper towels to help drain. Repeat to fry all your arancini.

Serve as they are, or with marinara sauce, vegan Parmesan, and basil, if you like.

Pie, Mashed Potatoes, and Liquor

☺ x 3

For the pies

2 teaspoons vegetable oil

1 onion, finely chopped

2 shiitake mushrooms, finely chopped

14oz (400g) chilled store-bought vegan ground beef

7 tablespoons boiling water

2 teaspoons massel beef stock powder, or vegan mushroom bouillon powder

1 teaspoon Marmite

1 teaspoon dark brown soy sauce

1 teaspoon vegan Worcestershire sauce (I use mushroom ketchup or Henderson's Relish)

½ teaspoon finely chopped parsley leaves

2 teaspoons cornstarch

1¼ cups (300ml) vegetable stock

1¼ cups (150g) self-rising flour, plus more to dust

2½oz (75g) shredded vegetable suet

6 tablespoons cold water

Vegan butter, for the pans

13oz (375g) ready-rolled vegan puff pastry

2 tablespoons soy milk

Fine sea salt and freshly ground black pepper

Malt vinegar or chili vinegar, to serve

⇨

If you're looking for a decent vegan pie, I'm your guy! I spent my teens around the village of Wigan (where people are literally known as "Pie Eaters") and my twenties in East London (home of the East End pie shop). This makes me essentially a feral child, raised by pies... aaah, marvel at his slightly crusty exterior! This recipe is based on the pies from M Manze's in London, a pie shop that's been around for well over a hundred years. Traditionally, the pies were filled with beef, or eels fished from the Thames, and served with a "liquor" made from fish stock and parsley. For this recipe, I suggest using store-bought vegan ground beef (the chilled rather than the frozen kind) because it's the meatiest out there, and I've given the liquor a seafood vibe with the addition of kombu seaweed.

Place a saucepan over medium heat with the oil. When hot, add the onion and fry for 5 minutes, stirring, until light brown. Add the mushrooms and ground meat and fry for 2 minutes. Add the boiling water, stock powder, Marmite, soy sauce, mushroom ketchup, ½ teaspoon pepper, and parsley and bring to a simmer.

In a bowl, whisk the cornstarch and stock. Add to the filling, stirring. Cook until thickened, then transfer to a baking sheet, spreading the mixture out so the mixture cools quickly.

Next, make the suet pastry. Preheat the oven to 325°F (160°C) convection and place a baking sheet in the middle. Place the flour, suet, and ½ teaspoon salt in a bowl and add the cold water. Mix briefly until you have formed a coarse dough. Turn out and knead on a floured work surface for 5 minutes, then cover and set aside for 5 minutes.

Butter 3 individual foil pie pans. Lightly flour a work surface and unwrap the suet pastry. Roll it out into a ⅛in (2.5mm)-thick layer that should be big enough in surface area to line the 3 pans. Place a pie pan upside down on the pastry and use a knife to cut out an oval about ½in (1cm) bigger than the rim of the pan. Repeat twice more. These will form the bottom crusts of the pies.

Unroll the puff pastry and repeat the process, this time cutting the pastry the same size as the rim of the pan, to form the tops of the pies.

Line all 3 pans with the suet pastry, pushing into the corners. Fill with the cooled filling, then brush the lip of the pastry with a little water. Top with the puff pastry and pinch the 2 pastries together to seal.

Dinner:
Date Night

For the mashed potatoes

1¾lb (800g) Russet potatoes, peeled and halved

2 tablespoons soy milk

1½ tablespoons Vegan Butter (see page 272), or store-bought vegan butter

For the liquor

9oz (250ml) vegetable stock

⅝in (1.5cm) piece kombu

Leaves from small bunch parsley, finely chopped

2 tablespoons all-purpose flour

2 tablespoons cold water

Place the pans in a baking pan and fill with just-boiled water to reach halfway up. Cover the whole pan with foil. Bake for 30 minutes, then remove the pans from the pan. Empty the pan of its water and return to the oven. Increase the oven temperature to 400°F (200°C) convection.

Brush the pies all over with the soy milk, then return them to sit in the hot pan. Bake for 20–25 minutes more.

Meanwhile, to make the mashed potatoes, fill a large saucepan with boiling water, salt it well, and place over medium heat. Add the potatoes and boil for about 15 minutes, or until fork-tender.

Drain the potatoes in a colander and leave there to steam-dry for 5 minutes. Transfer to a large bowl and add the remaining mashed potato ingredients and a pinch of salt. Mash until smooth, then cover and set aside.

For the liquor, pour the stock into a medium saucepan and add the kombu. Place over medium heat

and bring to a boil. As soon as the stock boils, remove the kombu and discard.

Add the parsley and reduce the heat to low. Cover with a lid and leave to simmer for 5 minutes.

Meanwhile, in a small bowl, whisk the flour and cold water. While whisking, add the flour mixture to the hot stock. It should thicken quickly. With the heat still on low, allow the liquor to simmer for a few minutes more.

When the pies are baked, remove from the oven and allow to cool for a few minutes before removing from their pans.

Divide the potatoes and pies among 3 warmed plates and spoon over some liquor. Serve with malt vinegar or chili vinegar.

**Dinner:
Date Night**

Level ① ⟨2⟩

Birria Tacos

 x 4

For the sauce

2 dried ancho chilies,
   seeded and stemmed
1 dried guajillo chili,
   seeded and stemmed
3 garlic cloves, peeled
1 onion, halved
3 tomatoes, halved
¼ teaspoon cumin seeds
½ teaspoon black
   peppercorns
½ teaspoon cilantro seeds
½ cinnamon stick
2 bay leaves
1 teaspoon paprika
½ teaspoon dried oregano
1 tablespoon light brown
   sugar
¼ cup (60ml) white wine
   vinegar
1¼ cups (300ml) vegetable
   stock
⅔ cup (160ml) refined
   coconut oil (see recipe
   note on page 156)
Sea salt flakes

For the jackfruit

1 tablespoon olive oil
2 x 20oz (565g) cans young
   green jackfruit, drained

My dad has this thing where he can't eat anything that might make his fingers sticky or messy. He gets all squirmy and panicky at the mere thought of an over-filled jam sandwich. I'm telling you this as a word of warning: if you're like my dad in this regard, skip this recipe, run as fast as your little legs will carry you and don't stop to look back. The whole point of birria tacos is that they're saucy, messy, and all the more tasty because of it. My recipe uses pulled jackfruit to replace the traditional goat meat, and just wait until you taste that sauce.

To make the sauce, place the dried chilies, garlic, onion, tomatoes, cumin seeds, black peppercorns, cilantro seeds, cinnamon stick, and bay leaves in a medium saucepan for which you have a lid and add enough boiling water to just cover everything. Place over medium heat and bring to a boil, then reduce the heat to a simmer and cover with the lid. Leave to simmer for 10 minutes.

Drain the water through a fine-meshed sieve and transfer everything else to a blender. Add all the remaining sauce ingredients, except the coconut oil, with 1½ teaspoons salt, then blend until very smooth.

Transfer to a large casserole dish or an ovenproof saucepan with a lid. Place over low heat to keep warm while you prepare the jackfruit.

Preheat the oven to 400°F (200°C) convection. Place a large frying pan for which you have a lid over medium heat and add the olive oil. When hot, add the jackfruit and fry for a few minutes, stirring often until lightly browned on the outside. Be careful not to break up the chunks of jackfruit.

Remove from the heat and add the cooked jackfruit to the sauce. Top the sauce with the coconut oil, cover with the lid, and place in the hot oven to cook for 30–40 minutes, or until the sauce has reduced and is thick and glossy.

Dinner:
Date Night

Level ① ② ③

Birria Tacos

For the salsa
1 red onion, finely chopped
2 tomatoes, finely chopped
Juice 1 lime
Leaves from small bunch
    cilantro, finely chopped

To serve
24 corn tortillas
14oz (400g) Vegan
    Mozzarella (see page
    252), or store-bought
    vegan melting cheese

While the jackfruit cooks, in a bowl, combine all the salsa ingredients with a pinch of salt and mix together. Chill until ready to serve.

Remove the jackfruit sauce from the oven. Use a slotted spoon to transfer the cooked jackfruit from the sauce to a separate baking sheet. Use 2 forks to pull the jackfruit into shreds.

Place a medium frying pan over medium heat. Take a corn tortilla and dip one side into the top of the sauce (which should have a layer of the coconut oil on the surface). Place dipped-side down in the hot frying pan.

Spread half the tortilla with vegan mozzarella (or sprinkle, if using store-bought cheese). Top with some shredded jackfruit and a few teaspoons salsa. Fold over the tortilla and flip to fry the other side until the cheese has melted and the tortilla is lightly crispy.

Remove from the frying pan and serve with a side of the sauce. Repeat until all your tortillas have run out (or until you're pleasantly full).

> **Recipe note**
> It can feel odd adding the refined coconut oil to the jackfruit stew, but trust me on this. When made with meat, the stew ends up with a layer of fat on the surface that you dunk your tortillas into before frying. We're doing the same thing, but we're getting our fat from plants instead.

Chorizo and Sundried Tomato Gnocchi Bake

☺ × 2

1 tablespoon olive oil

1 onion, finely chopped

2 garlic cloves, crushed or finely grated

6 sundried tomatoes, finely chopped

5½oz (150g) Seitan Chorizo (see page 240), or vegan sausages, sliced into coins

14oz (400g) can chopped tomatoes

1¼ cups (300ml) vegetable stock

1 teaspoon dried oregano

1½lb (700g) fresh gnocchi (make sure it's vegan)

3½oz (100g) Vegan Mozzarella (see page 252), or vegan melting cheese

Leaves from small bunch parsley or basil, torn, or baby herb leaves

Most fresh store-bought gnocchi is vegan, which is fabulous, because it leaves us with more time to get excited about the sauce! The bulk of the flavor in this dish comes from my Seitan Chorizo, so if you decide to skip making your own and buy a store-bought variety instead, make sure you pick a tasty one!

Preheat the oven to 400°F (200°C) convection.

Place a large, ovenproof saucepan over medium heat and add the olive oil. When hot, add the onion and garlic. Fry for 3 minutes, but do not allow to brown. Add the sundried tomatoes along with the seitan chorizo or sausages and fry for 1 minute more.

Add the chopped tomatoes, stock, oregano, and gnocchi. Stir to combine. Bring to a simmer, then cover with a lid and allow to cook for 10 minutes, stirring occasionally. Transfer to the oven to bake for 15 minutes.

Remove the lid and top with the vegan mozzarella. Return to the oven without the lid and bake for 5–10 minutes more or until the cheese is golden brown and bubbling.

Top with the herb leaves to serve.

Dinner:
Date Night

Level ① ⟨2⟩ ⟨3⟩

Hasselback Lancashire Hotpot

☺ x 4

1½lb (700g) medium potatoes, peeled (Russets work best)
2 teaspoons Marmite
2 tablespoons dark soy sauce
2½ cups (600ml) boiling vegetable stock
7oz (200g) TVP chunks, or 21oz (600g) Seitan Chunks (see page 243)
2 tablespoons Vegan Butter (see page 272), or store-bought vegan butter
1 onion, coarsely chopped
3 carrots, coarsely chopped
2 celery ribs, coarsely chopped
¼ cup (30g) all-purpose flour
2 bay leaves
3½oz (100g) green beans, trimmed and coarsely chopped
2 tablespoons vegetable oil
Leaves from 2 thyme sprigs
Sea salt flakes and freshly ground black pepper

Equipment needed
Mandoline

Lancashire hotpot with a couple of extra frills around the gills: imagine a hearty stew wearing an Elizabethan ruff and you're on the right track. But stacking the sliced potatoes on their sides instead of flat isn't just for aesthetics. It encourages some next-level crispy action, and show me anyone who's mad at a crispy spud!

Preheat the oven to 325°F (165°C) convection.

Fill a large bowl with cold water. Use a mandoline to slice the potatoes into thin disks—ideally ⅛in (3mm)—transferring them to the water as soon as they're sliced. Set aside.

In a bowl, whisk together the Marmite, soy sauce, and boiling stock. Add the TVP chunks, if using, cover with a plate, and leave to hydrate for at least 20 minutes. If using seitan chunks, just combine the Marmite, soy sauce, and stock and set aside.

Place a large, ovenproof pot or casserole dish for which you have a lid over medium heat and add the vegan butter. When melted, add the onion, and fry for a minute, or until softening.

Add the carrots and celery and fry for another minute or 2. If using TVP, drain it, reserving the liquid. Add the hydrated, drained TVP, or the seitan chunks to the frying vegetables. Stir well and cook for 5 minutes more, allowing the TVP or seitan chunks to brown lightly.

Add the flour and stir to coat everything. Add the reserved stock mixture, bay leaves, and just enough water to cover. Stir again, add the green beans, and season to taste. Cover with a lid and bring to a simmer, stirring occasionally until the sauce has thickened into a rich gravy.

Drain the sliced potatoes and carefully pat dry with a clean dish towel. Remove the hotpot from the heat. Carefully arrange the sliced potatoes on their sides in a fanned-out spiral across the top of the stew.

Drizzle the top of the potatoes with the vegetable oil, sprinkle with salt and pepper, and cover with the lid.

Place in the oven to bake for 45 minutes before removing the lid and returning to the oven for 30 minutes more, or until the top is crispy and golden.

Sprinkle with thyme and serve.

**Dinner:
Date Night**

Level ① ②

Family Meals and Party Food

"From now on, you'll be turning up to every party equipped with a piping hot tray of vegan joy for all to share!"

Let's role-play: you're newly vegan and you're invited to a birthday party. This should be a time of joy, but, instead, you're starting to get the wiggins! Will there be vegan food? Should I take my own canapés? Will anyone even notice my Spice Girls T-shirt? Suddenly, out of nowhere, I'm there, standing next to you. How did I get into your house? Shhh. That doesn't matter right now. You take a deep breath as I pick up this book and flick to this very chapter: problem solved!

I've stuffed the next few pages chock-full with ideas for vegan party food and big slap-up family dinners that will banish your food dread once and for all. From now on, you'll be turning up to every party equipped with a piping hot tray of vegan joy for all to share!

Vegan Agony Aunt

What do you cook for a vegan dinner party to impress non-vegans?
A lot of people encounter this experience and assume it's their job (as a vegan) to convince non-vegans to give up meat and dairy. In reality, that's not your problem. If you're cooking for someone, cook from the heart and make sure you love what you're serving. As with anything else, when your passion shines through, people see that and want a piece of it (and a piece of what you cooked, too).

Family Meals
and Party Food

Blender Bean Burgers

Makes 8

14oz (400g) can black beans, drained

14oz (400g) can young green jackfruit, drained

1 teaspoon olive oil, plus more for cooking

½ red onion, finely chopped

2 garlic cloves, crushed or finely grated

2 tablespoons miso paste (any type is good here)

⅓ cup (50g) rolled oats

1 teaspoon smoked paprika

2 tablespoons vegan gravy granules

1 tablespoon Marmite

Sea salt flakes and freshly ground black pepper

Grill-friendly burgers whipped up from a few vegan pantry ingredients? Is this another one of your schoolboy pranks, Richard Makin? No! It's not! It's real life and maybe you should be less suspicious about receiving delicious-looking vegan burgers? I'm just saying, when have I let you down? I even made sure this recipe doesn't do that squelchy mushy thing that most bean burgers do (the trick is to roast the beans to dry them out lightly). Now, why not sit down and enjoy your burger on this chair that's definitely not got a whoopee cushion on it.

Preheat the oven to 300°F (150°C) convection and line a baking sheet with parchment paper. Spread the drained black beans out on the baking sheet and place in the oven for 10–15 minutes, or until most of the beans have burst and appear dry. Remove from the oven and allow to cool fully.

Place the drained jackfruit in a nut-milk bag, or a sheet of muslin or cheesecloth, and squeeze out as much moisture as you can. Transfer to a bowl and use a fork to mash the jackfruit into coarse fibers with no chunks.

Heat a medium frying pan over medium heat and add the olive oil. Once hot, add both the onion and garlic and fry for 2–5 minutes, or until softened but not browned. Remove from the pan and leave to cool fully.

Place the beans, onion and garlic, miso paste, oats, paprika, gravy granules, and Marmite in a blender and pulse-blend until chunky and just combined. Transfer the blended mixture to the bowl with the jackfruit and mix together well.

Lightly wet your hands and form the burgers into thin hamburger patties; you should get around 8.

If cooking on a barbecue, brush the burgers with olive oil before grilling and sprinkle generously with salt and pepper. If cooking in a frying pan, brush the pan with a little olive oil and bring to medium heat. Sprinkle the burgers generously with salt and pepper and cook for 3–5 minutes on each side until nicely browned.

Serve in a soft bun with your favorite sauces and toppings, or double up with 2 slices vegan cheese if you want to serve double cheeseburgers.

Family Meals and Party Food

Level

Cauliflower Cheese Croquettes

Makes 15–20

For the filling

1 large head cauliflower

⅔ cup (160ml) soy milk

3 tablespoons tapioca flour/
starch

4 tablespoons nutritional
yeast

1 tablespoon English
mustard

1 tablespoon white miso
paste

3½ tablespoons Vegan
Butter (see page 272),
or store-bought vegan
butter

¼ cup (30g) all-purpose
flour

3 scallions, finely chopped,
plus more to serve

Fine sea salt and freshly
ground black pepper

Whatever your trauma is around cauliflower cheese, I'm here to fix it with a nice portion of deep-fried exposure therapy. Yes, I too had some dark experiences with cauliflower in the 1990s, but the therapy is working and I haven't had a flashback in months. These crispy boys are an entirely different experience from the sloppy casseroles and bakes of yesteryear and are guaranteed to create a cauliflower fan out of anyone.

To make the filling, bring a large saucepan of water to a boil. Trim the outer leaves from the cauliflower, cut off the end of the stem, and break the rest into florets. Place the florets in the boiling water and cook for 5–10 minutes, or until tender. Drain and set aside to cool for a few minutes.

Once cool enough to handle, chop half of the florets into chunks and place in a large bowl. Using the coarse holes of a box grater, grate the remaining florets into the same bowl. Transfer the cauliflower to a nut-milk bag and squeeze out as much water as you can manage. If you don't have a nut-milk bag, transfer to a sieve and use a spoon to push out the moisture.

Place the soy milk, tapioca flour, nutritional yeast, English mustard, white miso, ½ teaspoon salt, and ¼ teaspoon pepper in a blender. Blend until smooth, then cover and set aside.

Put the vegan butter into a medium saucepan and place over medium heat. Once melted,

whisk in the flour. Allow the flour to cook, constantly whisking, for about 1 minute, then slowly pour in the blended soy milk mixture.

While whisking constantly, cook the mixture until dramatically thickened and stringy. Remove from the heat and stir in the cauliflower and scallions. Transfer the mixture to a baking sheet and spread out evenly. Leave it to cool completely to room temperature.

Once cooled, spread around ¼ cup of the mixture in a rough line onto a sheet of plastic wrap. Wrap it up tightly into a small sausage shape, twisting both ends. Repeat the process with the remaining mixture, creating as many little sausages as possible before the mixture runs out (you should get 15–20). Once all the mixture is wrapped, transfer to the freezer for 1 hour.

**Family Meals
and Party Food**

Level ① ② ③

Cauliflower Cheese Croquettes

To coat and fry
1¾ cups (200g) all-purpose
    flour
⅔ cup (160ml) soy milk
1 cup (100g) golden bread
    crumbs
2 tablespoons nutritional
    yeast
Vegetable oil, for deep-frying
Sea salt flakes, to serve
Blender Ranch (see page
    263), or your favorite
    Quick Sauces (see pages
    260–270), to serve

Equipment needed
Meat thermometer

To coat and fry, place the flour in a small bowl, the soy milk in a separate small bowl, and the bread crumbs, nutritional yeast, and ¼ teaspoon salt in a third, mixing together the bread crumb ingredients to combine.

Remove a wrapped portion of the cauliflower mixture from the freezer and unwrap. Roll carefully in the flour, then coat in the soy milk, and, finally, in the bread crumbs. Set aside on a baking sheet. Repeat until all the croquettes are coated.

Fill a deep saucepan with at least 3in (7.5cm) vegetable oil and use a meat thermometer to bring the temperature to 340°F (170°C).

(Alternatively, use a deep-fat fryer and bring it to the same temperature.)

Fry the croquettes in batches of 3–5 (depending on the size of your saucepan) for 3–4 minutes. Remove once golden brown and drain on paper towels. Sprinkle with sea salt flakes and sliced scallions before serving with your favorite dip.

Family Meals
and Party Food

Level

No-Knead Pepperoni Pizza Al Taglio

Makes 2

Photographed on page 173

Whoever first came up with the idea of selling pizza by weight deserves some kind of medal. Ordering a kilo of pizza sounds weird, but in Rome, it's super common. Pizza al taglio is made in big metal trays, sliced with scissors and sold per kilo or 100g. For the pepperoni, we're using paper tofu (the same stuff I use to make bacon, see page 249) which actually cups like real pepperoni when drizzled with a little oil before baking.

For the pepperoni

2 sheets paper tofu
1 tablespoon dark soy sauce
1 tablespoon beet juice (from a store-bought vacuum-pack of roast beets)
2 tablespoons liquid smoke
2 tablespoons vegetable oil
2 teaspoons light brown sugar
1 tablespoon smoked paprika
Pinch cayenne pepper
Pinch allspice
Fine sea salt and freshly ground black pepper

For the dough

1⅓ cups (325ml) lukewarm water
1 teaspoon easy bake yeast
½ teaspoon sugar
2½ cups (250g) pizza flour, plus more to dust
2 cups (250g) white bread flour
1 tablespoon extra-virgin olive oil, plus more for the baking sheets

To make the pepperoni, unfold the sheets of paper tofu and place on a cutting board. Use the large end of a piping nozzle or a small cookie cutter to cut out as many 1in (2.5cm) circles of paper tofu as you can. Place in a shallow bowl.

In a measuring cup, whisk together the remaining pepperoni ingredients with ½ teaspoon pepper and pour over the paper tofu. Cover and leave to marinate while you make the dough and sauce.

For the dough, pour the lukewarm water into a bowl and add the yeast and sugar. Whisk well to combine and set aside for a few minutes until the mixture has developed a foamy surface.

Place the flours and 1 teaspoon salt into a large bowl, or the bowl of a stand mixer fitted with the paddle attachment. Add the yeast mixture and olive oil and mix together just until a coarse dough forms. If using a stand mixer, mix on the slowest setting. Cover the bowl with a damp dish towel and leave to rest for 10 minutes.

Remove the dough from the bowl once rested and place on a work surface. Pinch a corner of the dough and fold over into the middle. Rotate 90° and repeat, folding and rotating a total of 4 times. Flip the dough so it's seam-sides down and return to the bowl. Cover and leave to prove for 1 hour at room temperature, or place in the fridge overnight.

Once proofed, transfer the dough to a work surface. Gently push out the larger air bubbles with your fingers and use a sharp knife to slice it into 2 equal pieces.

Working with 1 piece of dough at a time, repeat the dough-folding process, pinching and folding the dough corners into the center. Flip the dough and place seam-sides down on a deep, lightly floured baking sheet. Repeat with the second piece of dough. Cover with a damp dish towel and leave to proof again for 1 hour.

Family Meals and Party Food

Level ① ②

For the sauce
2 x 14oz (400g) cans whole
    San Marzano tomatoes
2 teaspoons olive oil
3 garlic cloves, crushed
2 teaspoons sugar
½ teaspoon dried oregano

For topping
1 quantity Vegan Mozzarella
    (see page 252), or 7oz
    (200g) store-bought
    vegan melting cheese
Pinch dried oregano
2 teaspoons extra-virgin
    olive oil

Meanwhile, open the cans of tomatoes. Over a bowl, remove the tomatoes from the can, one by one, and squeeze in your hand so they form a chunky pulp. Leave the tomato sauce behind in the can for use in another recipe (always good in a pasta sauce, see page 270).

Place a medium saucepan over medium-low heat with the olive oil. Once hot, add the garlic and fry for around 30 seconds, making sure it doesn't brown or burn.

Add the chunky tomato pulp, sugar, and oregano with 1 teaspoon salt. Bring to a simmer, then leave to cook, stirring occasionally, for 15 minutes. When done, the sauce should be slightly thicker and darker. Season with pepper to taste.

Now to make the pizzas. Preheat the broiler and place a pizza stone or your thickest baking sheet on the top shelf. Oil 2 x 10in (25cm) square metal roasting pans or brownie pans with olive oil.

Turn one portion of the dough onto a work surface. Lightly wet your fingertips with water and push out any large air bubbles. Stretch the dough gently into a square roughly the same size as the pan. Transfer the dough to the pan and carefully push it right into the corners. If the dough resists, cover the pan with a damp dish towel and allow to rest for 5 minutes before trying again. Repeat with the second portion of dough and the other oiled pan.

Divide the tomato sauce between the 2 pans. Use a wet teaspoon to scoop up the vegan mozzarella and spread over the pizzas. Drain the marinated tofu pepperoni and divide it between the pizzas. Top with the dried oregano and a drizzle of extra-virgin olive oil.

Working with 1 pizza at a time, place the pan on top of the pizza stone or thickest baking pan under the broiler and broil for 10–15 minutes, rotating halfway through. Slice and serve immediately, while you repeat to bake the second pizza.

**Family Meals
and Party Food**

Level ① ② ③

Cajun Fried Shrimp with Rémoulade

Makes 20

I'm a lover, not a fighter, but if there's one recipe in this book that I would full-speed rugby tackle out of your hands, it's this one. You've probably got the picture by now that I love a big bowl of fried stuff with a dip on the side, but these mushroom-based vegan shrimp have got an extra-special place in my heart.

For the rémoulade
½ cup (120ml) Ten-Second Mayo (see page 262), or store-bought vegan mayo
1 tablespoon ketchup
1 tablespoon wholegrain mustard
1 teaspoon lemon juice
1 garlic clove, crushed or finely grated
1 tablespoon vegan horseradish cream
1 teaspoon hot sauce
1 teaspoon vegan Worcestershire sauce, or mushroom ketchup
¼ teaspoon Cajun seasoning

For the shrimp
5 king oyster mushrooms
1 cup (100g) all-purpose flour
Sunflower oil, for deep-frying
Lemon wedges, to serve

For the batter
1 tablespoon gram flour
1 teaspoon cold-pressed rapeseed oil
⅓ cup (85ml) soy milk
1 tablespoon hot sauce
1 tablespoon English mustard
2 teaspoons Cajun seasoning

For the dry coating
¾ cup (100g) cornmeal (aka polenta)
1 cup (100g) all-purpose flour
2 teaspoons Cajun seasoning

Equipment needed
Meat thermometer

To make the rémoulade, place all the ingredients into an empty jar and mix well. Seal with the lid and refrigerate until needed.

For the shrimp, cut the flat tops and bottoms off the king oyster mushrooms and store for use in a different recipe. Trim each stem to a 3in- (7.5cm-) long cylinder, then slice into quarters lengthwise.

Place in a heatproof bowl and cover with just-boiled water. Now cover with a plate and leave to soften for 5 minutes.

Drain the mushrooms and leave to cool for a few minutes, then return to a dry bowl. Add the flour and toss to coat all sides of the mushrooms.

Take a strip of mushroom and bend into a shrimp shape, threading a toothpick through to keep it in place. Repeat with the remaining pieces of mushroom until you have 20 shrimps on toothpicks.

Fill a medium saucepan with 2–3in (5–7.5cm) sunflower oil and place over medium heat until it reaches 340°F (170°C) on a meat thermometer. Alternatively, fill and turn on a deep-fat fryer to 340°F (170°C).

In a bowl, whisk together the batter ingredients. Set aside. In a separate bowl, mix together the dry coating ingredients.

Carefully dip the shrimp into the batter, then transfer to the dry mixture to coat.

Carefully lower the shrimp into the hot oil in batches of 5. Remove from the oil when crispy and lightly browned and drain on paper towels. Repeat to deep-fry the remaining shrimp. Carefully remove the skewers, if you like, or at least warn your guests they are there!

Serve hot with the rémoulade, and lemon wedges for squeezing.

Cheeseburger Sausage Rolls

Makes 10

For the quick tomato relish

1 tablespoon olive oil

½ red onion, finely chopped

2 garlic cloves, crushed or finely grated

¾lb (350g) ripe tomatoes, finely chopped

3 tablespoons white wine vinegar

¼ cup (50g) sugar

Fine sea salt and freshly ground black pepper

For the sausage rolls

3 store-bought vegan burgers (total weight around ¾lb [340g])

1 onion, finely chopped

4 gherkins, finely chopped

13oz (370g) package ready-rolled vegan puff pastry

4 slices vegan burger cheese, finely chopped, or 1 quantity Vegan Mozzarella (see page 252)

2 tablespoons soy milk

2 tablespoons white sesame seeds

Simple, rustic, and undeniably heart-warming. But enough about me, get a load of these sausage rolls! Every year on Christmas morning we wrap up my nan (aka Nanny Dartboard) in every coat we own, so she can't bend her arms, and head to the woods for Sausagemas. We fill cups with mulled apple juice and get the day started properly with freshly baked vegan sausage rolls. These fellas are Nanny Dartboard's favorite, because of the tomato relish inside, which keeps things sweet and tangy like a cheeseburger.

To make the relish, place a medium saucepan over medium-low heat and add the olive oil. When hot, add the red onion and garlic and fry for a minute or 2, but do not allow to brown.

Add all the remaining ingredients and stir to combine. Reduce the heat to low and simmer for 10 minutes, stirring regularly. Season with ½ teaspoon salt and a pinch of pepper, remove from the heat, and allow to cool completely.

Preheat the oven to 400°F (200°C) convection and line a baking sheet with parchment paper.

For the sausage roll filling, place the burgers, chopped onion, and gherkins into a small bowl and add a pinch of salt and ½ teaspoon pepper. Mash with your hands until combined and no longer burger-shaped. Set aside.

Unroll the pastry and slice it lengthwise down the center to create 2 long strips. Down the center of each strip, again lengthwise, spread one-quarter of the relish (keep the remaining relish for serving), leaving around ½in (1cm) gap on each long edge. Sprinkle (or spread) the vegan cheese over the relish, dividing it equally between the 2 rolls, and top with a few extra grinds of pepper.

Add half of the hamburger mixture to each strip of pastry on top of the cheese, fold over the pastry to enclose the filling, and seal the seam with a fork. Brush the top with the soy milk and sprinkle with the sesame seeds.

Transfer the long rolls to the lined baking sheet and use a sharp knife to slice each into 5 sausage rolls.

Bake for 25 minutes or until puffed up and golden. Serve with the reserved tomato relish.

Family Meals and Party Food

Level

King Oyster Mushroom Yakitori

Makes 6–8

King oysters are the Dwayne Johnson of the mushroom kingdom. They're really meaty, actually super nice, and also very interesting to look at in a purely scientific kind of way. That's why I've chosen to use them in this yakitori recipe. The shrooms are sliced superthin and woven on to a skewer before being grilled and basted with Japanese tare sauce. Bingo! The perfect veg side for a big family barbecue.

For the yakitori

7oz (200g) (around 6 large) king oyster mushrooms

1 tablespoon vegetable oil, plus more for cooking

For the tare sauce

7 tablespoons (100ml) soy sauce

7 tablespoons (100ml) mirin

3½ tablespoons (50ml) sake

3½ tablespoons (50ml) water

2 tablespoons coconut sugar, or light brown sugar

2 teaspoons rice vinegar

2 garlic cloves, chopped

2 scallions, coarsely chopped

⅝in (1.5cm) piece ginger peeled and chopped

Place 6–8 bamboo skewers in a bowl and cover with water. Leave them to soak for at least 1 hour.

Use a mandoline to slice the king oyster mushroom stems into long, ¼in- (5mm-) thick strips. Transfer to a bowl and cover with just-boiled water. Leave to soften for 5 minutes, then drain the water.

Once the drained mushrooms are cool enough to handle, drizzle with the vegetable oil. Use your hands to mix and make sure everything is lightly coated.

Take a strip of king oyster mushroom, fold it repeatedly like an accordion, and skewer it through the center to keep it in place. Repeat until the skewer is full, then move on to the next until all the mushrooms are skewered.

If you're planning to cook the yakitori on a barbecue, fire it up now. Make sure the grill or wire rack you plan to place the skewers on is lightly oiled to prevent sticking.

Place the tare sauce ingredients in a small saucepan and whisk well to combine. Place over medium heat and bring to a boil. Reduce the heat to low and simmer until the sauce is reduced by half and is thick and glossy. Remove from the heat, strain, and set aside.

Arrange the yakitori on the wire rack and place on the barbecue. Grill until lightly browned, then flip and repeat on the other side (4–5 minutes on each side). Alternatively, place a large frying pan over medium heat and drizzle with a little oil. Fry the king oyster yakitori for around 5 minutes on each side, or until lightly browned.

Brush the yakitori with the tare sauce and place back on the barbecue or in the frying pan. Cook for 2 minutes before flipping, brushing with the sauce again and repeating. Repeat this process twice more, brushing with more sauce each time.

Once fully grilled and coated in caramelized, sticky sauce, the yakitori are ready to serve, with lime slices, radishes, and cilantro on the side, if you like.

Family Meals and Party Food

Level

Charred Corn Elotes with Miso Crema

Makes 4

4 ears corn

7 tablespoons Vegan Butter (see page 272), or store-bought vegan butter, melted

2 tablespoons white miso paste

¼ cup (60g) Ten-Second Mayo (see page 262), or store-bought vegan mayo

2 tablespoons soy milk, at room temperature

1 tablespoon lime juice, plus lime wedges to serve

1 tablespoon vegetable oil

7oz (200g) Grateable Parmesan (see page 255), or store-bought vegan Parmesan, finely grated

Leaves from small bunch cilantro, finely chopped

1 tablespoon mild chili powder

I first tried corn elotes at a vegan Mexican street food pop-up by Club Mexicana in London. I took one bite and broke into a celebratory moonwalk, with hot sauce and crumbly vegan cheese smeared on my face. It's pretty safe to say that I've been trying to replicate that recipe ever since. My love for this version is all about the bitterness of that gentle char on the outside of the kernels, balanced with the sweetness of the miso crema. Traditional elotes are made with crumbly *cotija* cheese, so my Grateable Parmesan was a natural choice here. Oh, and be prepared to get messy: don't say I didn't warn you...

Shuck the ears of corn and discard the husks. Bring a large pot of water to a boil. Add the corn and boil for 5 minutes, then remove from the water and set aside to cool.

While the corn cools, place the vegan butter, miso, mayo, soy milk, and lime juice in a blender and blend until smooth to make the crema. Transfer to a bowl and set aside.

Once cooled, brush the corn with the vegetable oil and place on a hot grill. Cook the corn until the bottom is lightly charred, then rotate a little and repeat until the whole cob is lightly charred all around.

While hot, dunk and roll each corncob in the crema, then sprinkle liberally with the vegan Parmesan. Finally, top with the cilantro and a sprinkle of chili powder and serve hot, with lime wedges for squeezing.

Family Meals and Party Food

Level ① ② ⟨3⟩

Family Meals
and Party Food

Level ① ② ☆③☆

Vegan Sushi Sharing Platter

The idea of using eggplant as a substitute for unagi (Japanese eel) came from the Instagram feed of Lisa Kitahara, the genius behind @okonomikitchen. She made it look so good and so easy, I immediately did a little dry-cry with excitement. That eggplant unagi started a sushi-shaped chain reaction and we ended up here, with a table full of rolls and nigiri unlocked for vegan enjoyment!

King Oyster Mushroom Hirame Nigiri

Photographed on page 184

Makes 24

For the mushrooms
3 king oyster mushrooms
2in (5cm) piece of kombu
2 tablespoons vegan fish sauce, or soy sauce
1 tablespoon vegetable oil

For the nigiri sushi
2¼ cups (350g) cooked, seasoned sushi rice
Soy sauce, wasabi, and pickled ginger, to serve

Trim the tops and bottoms off the king oyster mushrooms and use a mandoline or vegetable peeler to slice them lengthwise into ¼in (5mm) slices. Place in a bowl and cover with just-boiled water, then add the kombu and vegan fish sauce. Set aside to soak for 10 minutes.

Drain the water and allow the mushrooms to cool briefly. Use a sharp knife to score shallow slashes diagonally down the length of each strip of mushroom on both sides, then place in a dry bowl.

Drizzle the scored mushroom strips with the vegetable oil, then very gently massage, to make sure all the strips are coated.

Heat a large frying pan over high heat. When very hot, add the strips of mushrooms in batches of 4 to avoid crowding the pan.

Fry until just browned before flipping and repeating, about 2 minutes on each side. Remove from the pan and repeat with the remaining mushroom strips.

Line a baking sheet with parchment paper. Lightly wet your hands with water and grab a small handful of the cooked sushi rice. Form into a long oval 2–2 ½in (5–6cm) in length, squeezing the rice as you go, to make sure it's firmly packed.

Carefully drape a strip of mushroom over each oval of rice. Wet your hands lightly and give each nigiri a little squeeze to perfect their shape (see photo on page 184). Serve with soy sauce, wasabi, and pickled ginger.

Eggplant Unagi Nigiri

Makes 24

Photographed on page 184

For the sauce
7 tablespoons soy sauce
7 tablespoons mirin
1 tablespoon sake
2 tablespoon light brown sugar

For the eggplant unagi
2 long, thin eggplants (aka Japanese eggplants)
¼ cup (60ml) vegetable oil, plus more for the pan

For the nigiri sushi
2¼ cups (350g) cooked, seasoned sushi rice
2 sheets unseasoned nori
2 tablespoons white sesame seeds
Soy sauce, wasabi, and pickled ginger, to serve

Put all the sauce ingredients into a small saucepan and place over medium heat. Bring to a boil, stirring occasionally. Let simmer for about 5 minutes, or until the volume has reduced by half, then turn off the heat and allow to cool completely.

For the unagi, preheat the broiler.

Trim the tops off the eggplants, slice in half lengthwise, and use a fork to prick a few holes in the skins. Fill a medium saucepan halfway with water and top with a bamboo steamer. Place the eggplants in the steamer and steam for 20 minutes.

Remove the eggplants from the steamer and allow to cool for a few minutes. Place flat-sides down on a cutting board and slice each half into 4 strips lengthwise. Working with 1 strip of eggplant at a time, use a sharp knife to gently score diagonal lines across the white flesh, then slice into nigiri-size pieces.

Place on a lightly oiled baking sheet and brush with the vegetable oil. Place under the broiler. Broil for about 5 minutes on each side, or until gently charred.

Remove from under the broiler and brush both sides with some unagi sauce. Return to the broiler for a few minutes more before removing and brushing again with unagi sauce. Remove and set aside to cool.

Line a baking sheet with parchment paper. Lightly wet your hands with water and grab a small handful of the cooked sushi rice. Form into a long oval 2–2 ½in (5–6cm) in length, squeezing the rice as you go, to make sure it's firmly packed.

Divide each sheet of nori into 12 long, thin strips. Take 1 strip of nori and place it shiny-side down on a dry work surface.

Next, place a piece of eggplant across the center of the nori (see photo, on page 184). Finally, place an oval of rice on top of the eggplant and wrap the ends of the nori strip around the rice. If necessary, seal the strip in place with a little water.

Flip the piece of nigiri so the eggplant is now on the top. Set aside on a plate. Repeat the process with the remaining 23 ovals of rice and pieces of eggplant.

Once all the nigiri are assembled, brush the top with a little unagi sauce and sprinkle with sesame seeds. Serve with the soy sauce, wasabi, and pickled ginger.

Family Meals and Party Food

Level

Spicy Crab Roll

Makes 16

For the spicy crab salad

10oz (285g) extra-firm tofu

6 radishes

6 tablespoons Ten-Second Mayo see page 262), or store-bought vegan mayo

5 tablespoons sriracha sauce

For the sushi roll

2 sheets unseasoned nori

2¼ cups (350g) cooked, seasoned sushi rice

3 tablespoons white sesame seeds

½ cucumber (pick a perfectly straight one if you can), sliced into ¼in (5mm) batons

Soy sauce, wasabi, and pickled ginger, to serve

To make the salad, use a fine grater to shred the tofu into a bowl. Using the same grater, shred the radishes into the bowl. Add the mayo and sriracha. Mix carefully until well combined.

Lay out a sheet of nori on a piece of plastic wrap or a sushi mat. Lightly wet your fingers and spread half the cooked sushi rice over the entire sheet from edge to edge in an even layer. Sprinkle with half the sesame seeds.

Carefully pinch the top edges of the nori and flip it over so the rice is now touching the plastic wrap or sushi mat and the nori is facing up. Along the center, lay a horizontal line of the cucumber strips. On the side of the line of cucumber closest to you, spread a heaping line of the crab salad (be sure not to use more than half the crab salad).

Gently lift the nearest edge of the plastic wrap, wrapping the rice and nori over the crab salad and cucumber. Without squeezing too hard (or the crab salad will escape from the 2 ends), pinch the roll so it's nice and tight. Peel back the plastic wrap or sushi mat to reveal the rolled rice and gently continue to roll the sushi tightly.

Cover the completed roll again with the plastic wrap or sushi mat and gently squeeze along its length to make sure the roll is sealed. Remove the plastic wrap or sushi mat and place the roll to the side.

Repeat to form the second sushi roll.

Take your sharpest knife and dip it in hot water to prevent the rice from sticking. Slice the rolls in half at the middle point. Slice each half in 2, then do the same to each quarter so you end up with 8 pieces for each roll. Arrange on a plate. Serve with soy sauce, wasabi, and pickled ginger.

Sweet
Stuff

"A collection of all my favorite desserts on planet Earth, except made with plants."

This chapter is a collection of all my favorite desserts on planet Earth, except made with plants. Before School Night Vegan, my idea of a plant-based dessert was tainted by a particularly harrowing dessert I was served at a dinner party, back in university. It became known as "the dessert that shall not be named," largely because nobody actually knew what it was supposed to be, not even the guy who made it. There was carob-chocolate-substitute involved, but also jelly and some kind of upsetting pastry. When I reached the warm avocado mousse, I knew something was terribly wrong.

It took me years to realize that things have changed, people have grown, and perhaps that particular dessert was going through a rough day; we can't all be our best selves all of the time. So I gave some vegan desserts a try. Straight out of the gate, things were better than anticipated, and sometimes I achieved surprisingly delicious results by simply omitting the animal products. Other recipes were more complicated; finding egg replacements for sponge cake and cream replacements for ice cream became riddles I was determined to crack. But I persevered and, what's more, I loved the process. What follows is everything I figured out, shared freely with you, because vegans deserve dessert, too!

Palm Springs Date Shake

For the date caramel
10–15 large unpitted
    Medjool dates
¼ cup (50g) light brown
    sugar, unpacked
Pinch ground cinnamon
1 teaspoon vanilla extract

For the shakes
7oz (200g) vegan vanilla
    ice cream (for home-
    made, see page 219)
1¼ cups (300ml) full-fat
    oat milk
Vegan whipped cream, or
    whipped coconut cream,
    or my Vegan Whipped
    Cream (see page 196),
    to serve

The last non-vegan dessert I ever enjoyed was a date shake from Lappert's in Palm Springs. Date shakes are a bit of a cultural phenomenon in southern California, due to the abundance of date palms, and I think about them all the time. It's essentially a milkshake that's been swirled with a rich date caramel and topped with whipped cream. Oat milk is a must for any vegan version because it's just so damn creamy, and try to use the extra smooth "barista" variety if you can get hold of it.

To make the caramel, carefully remove and discard the pits from the dates. Place the dates in a small bowl. Cover with just-boiled water and cover the bowl. Leave to soak for 30 minutes. Drain the dates, but reserve 7 tablespoons of the soaking water.

Place the drained dates, reserved soaking water, light brown sugar, cinnamon, and vanilla in a blender. Blend until completely smooth.

Transfer the mixture to a medium saucepan and place over medium heat. Bring to a simmer, then reduce the heat to low. Allow to simmer for around 5 minutes, stirring often, until the mixture has reduced and thickened slightly. Remove the pan from the heat and leave to cool fully before transferring to the fridge in a sealed container. The date caramel will keep in the fridge for up to 2 weeks.

Chill 2 large shake glasses in the fridge for at least 10 minutes before making the shakes.

Decant 3 tablespoons of the date caramel into the bottom of each of the 2 chilled glasses.

Put the ice cream and oat milk into the blender with the remaining date caramel and blend until smooth.

Divide the blended shake mixture between the 2 glasses.

Top the shakes with the whipped cream and serve immediately.

Glossy Sea Salt Brownies

Makes 12

1½ cups (185g) all-purpose flour
6 tablespoons cocoa powder
1 teaspoon psyllium husk powder
½ teaspoon baking powder
1⅓ cups (220g) vegan dark chocolate chips, more than 70 percent cacao
3 tablespoons sunflower oil
1⅓ cups (285g) sugar
⅔ cup (150ml) water
1 teaspoon vanilla extract
Sea salt flakes

The last thing the world needs is another vegan brownie recipe, I know, but hear me out. Vegan brownies never seem to have that gorgeous, shiny, lacey layer on the top that cracks and fractures as you slice. For years, I assumed it was probably down to the egg whites or the butter fat or some other non-vegan element, but I was wrong. The key is to make sure that your sugar is completely dissolved in syrup form before adding it to the mix, then to quickly transfer the batter to the baking sheet before it has time to cool down and lose that glossy surface. Has anyone else ever spent this long studying brownies? Probably no. Is it worth it? Definitely yes!

Preheat the oven to 350°F (180°C) convection. Line a 10 x 7 ½in (25 x 19cm) brownie pan with parchment paper.

In a bowl, sift together the flour, cocoa, psyllium husk powder, and baking powder. Add a pinch of salt flakes and set aside.

Place a saucepan of water over medium heat and bring to a boil, then reduce the heat to a simmer. Place 4 ½oz (130g) of the dark chocolate chips and the sunflower oil in a heatproof bowl and place on top of the saucepan, making sure the water isn't touching the bowl. Stir occasionally, until the chocolate is completely melted, then remove the bowl from the saucepan and set aside.

In a second heatproof bowl, combine the sugar and water. Place over the simmering saucepan and stir constantly until the sugar is completely dissolved and you're left with a smooth syrup. Add the vanilla extract and remove the bowl from the pan.

While whisking constantly, pour the sugar syrup into the melted chocolate mixture. Continue whisking until you have a smooth, glossy mixture. While the mixture is still warm, add the flour mixture and the remaining dark chocolate chips and stir until completely combined.

Working quickly, pour the batter into the prepared brownie pan. Do not smooth out the surface. Place in the oven and bake for 20 minutes.

Remove from the oven and allow to cool completely before slicing and serving.

Level ① ② ③

Olive Oil Chocolate Chip Cookies

Makes 20

1⅓ cups (175g) all-purpose flour

½ teaspoon baking powder

½ teaspoon baking soda

7 tablespoons olive oil, at room temperature

¼ cup (50g) soft light brown sugar

¼ cup (50g) soft dark brown sugar

⅓ cup (70g) sugar

3 tablespoons soy milk

1 teaspoon vanilla extract

5½oz (155g) vegan dark chocolate chips or chunks, more than 70 percent cacao

1oz (30g) vegan dark chocolate squares, more than 70 percent cacao

Fine sea salt

Sea salt flakes

Store-bought vegan butter is frustratingly inconsistent in texture and flavor from one brand to the next. A cookie recipe may work with one brand of vegan margarine, but be a disaster with vegan block butter. My own vegan butter is obvs insanely good (says my mam) but it takes time to make and I wanted these cookies to be ready in a jiffy. As such, the development behind this recipe was like *The Twilight Zone*: "A Week of A Thousand Cookies." But, boy, did I crack it! Instead of vegan butter, this uses olive oil. It's consistent in texture, so this recipe is one hundred percent reliable. I'm also personally not mad at the gentle fruity flavor of olive oil in my cookies. It makes me feel posh and refined, which is why I eat these cookies with my pinkie finger sticking up.

Line a cookie sheet with parchment paper and set aside.

In a bowl, combine the flour, baking powder, baking soda, and ¼ teaspoon fine sea salt.

In the bowl of a stand mixer fitted with the paddle attachment, beat together the olive oil, all 3 sugars, the soy milk, and vanilla until the mixture resembles a smooth, pale caramel. If you don't have a stand mixer, use a handheld electric mixer instead.

Add the dry ingredients to the wet and stir until combined, being careful not to overmix. Add the chocolate chips and stir to combine. Cover the bowl and place in the fridge to chill for 1 hour.

Preheat the oven to 325°F (165°C) convection.

Using a cookie scoop, or a spoon, form balls of cookie dough around the size of a walnut and arrange them on the prepared sheet 2–3in (5–7.5cm) apart.

Break the chocolate squares into rough, ½–¾in (1–2cm) chunks and push a few into the top of each ball of cookie dough. Sprinkle with a small pinch of sea salt flakes and bake in the preheated oven for 16 minutes.

Once baked, carefully slide the parchment paper from the cookie sheet onto a wire rack and leave to cool for at least 20 minutes before serving.

> **Recipe note**
> If you can, use a good, tasty extra-virgin olive oil and a delicious bittersweet vegan chocolate. I'm also asking, nay, begging you to use two different types of chocolate in this recipe. The chips or chunks make sure the cookies are packed with chocolate, while the larger squares perch on the dough and form a big chocolatey archipelago across the top of each cookie once it's baked.

Chocolate Pretzel Pie

For the whipped cream

⅔ cup (135g) refined
  coconut oil
⅔ cup (145ml) lukewarm
  soy milk
¼ cup (25g) confectioners'
  sugar, sifted
½ teaspoon vanilla extract

For the crust

7 tablespoons Vegan Butter
  (see page 272), or store-
  bought vegan butter,
  melted, plus more for
  the pan
5½oz (150g) salted pretzels,
  finely crushed, plus more,
  coarsely crushed, to serve
¼ cup (50g) demerara sugar

Equipment needed

High-speed blender (optional)

Yes, this pie contains lots of chocolate and, yes, the crust is made from salty pretzels, but just hold your horses for a minute. The real element to get excited about is the vegan whipped cream on top. It's entirely homemade and doesn't involve any dubious cans of squirty cream. I figured out that if you blend together melted coconut oil and soy milk in proportions that mimic the fat content of heavy cream, you end up with an emulsion that whips just like heavy cream. As you can imagine, upon discovery, I screamed "EUREKA!" so loud I gave myself a migraine.

To make the whipped cream, place the coconut oil in a microwave-safe bowl. Melt the coconut oil in 10-second bursts in the microwave until just melted. If the oil gets hot, set aside to cool to just above room temperature.

Place the lukewarm soy milk and lukewarm coconut oil in the bowl of a high-speed blender. Blend until completely smooth and combined at the highest speed possible, remove and shake the cup, then blend again. Alternatively, place the ingredients in a tall container and blend with an immersion blender until very smooth. Place the cream in the fridge along with the bowl of a stand mixer, or a medium mixing bowl, to chill overnight.

Once the bowl and the cream are completely chilled, remove from the fridge. Pour/spoon the cream into the chilled mixing bowl and fit a stand mixer, if using, with the whisk attachment. Whip on medium speed until soft peaks form. Add the confectioners' sugar and vanilla, then whip again until stiff peaks form. Alternatively, whip it with a handheld electric mixer in the chilled bowl. Do not overwhip, or the cream will split.

Cover and place in the fridge while you make the pie.

For the crust, preheat the oven to 350°F (180°C) convection and lightly butter a 9in (23cm) pie pan.

In a bowl, place the crust ingredients and mix until thoroughly combined. Press the crust mixture evenly over both the bottom and sides of the pie pan and place in the oven to bake for 10 minutes. Allow to cool fully on a wire rack, then transfer to the fridge to chill.

Chocolate Pretzel Pie

For the filling

8oz (225g) vegan dark
  chocolate, more than 70
  percent cacao, broken up
¼ cup (50ml) refined
  coconut oil
8oz (225g) silken tofu
⅔ cup confectioners' sugar
½ cup (120ml) any plant milk
2 tablespoons cocoa powder
1 tablespoon espresso
  powder
Sea salt flakes

Equipment needed

High-speed blender (optional)

To make the filling, melt the chocolate and coconut oil together in a heatproof bowl set over a pan of gently simmering water, stirring frequently.

Put the silken tofu, confectioners' sugar, plant milk, cocoa powder, espresso powder, and a pinch of salt into a high-speed blender and blend until completely smooth. Add the melted chocolate mixture to the blender and blend again. Alternatively, place the ingredients in a tall container and blend with an immersion blender until very smooth.

Pour the mixture into the chilled crust and tap gently on the work surface to flatten the filling of the pie. Place in the fridge to chill and set for at least 3 hours.

When the pie is set, spoon the whipped cream on to the center. Top with crushed pretzels, slice, and serve.

Blackout Cake

Photographed
on page 201

🙂 x 8–12

For the chocolate custard

1¼ cups (250g) superfine
    sugar
2¼ cups (525ml) soy milk
5½oz (150g) vegan dark
    chocolate, ideally 55–60
    percent cacao, roughly
    chopped
7 tablespoons cornstarch
1 tablespoon cocoa powder
1 tablespoon espresso
    powder

For the cake

¾ cup (160g) Vegan Butter
    (see page 272), or store-
    bought vegan butter,
    melted, plus more for
    the pans
½ cup (120ml) vegetable oil
⅔ cup (160ml) soy milk
2 teaspoons rice vinegar
1 tablespoon espresso
    powder
1 teaspoon vanilla extract
1½ teaspoons psyllium husk
    powder
9½oz (270g) light brown
    sugar
½ cup (120ml) boiling water
2 cups (230g) all-purpose
    flour
1 teaspoon baking soda
2 teaspoons baking powder
⅞ cup (80g) cocoa powder
Fine sea salt

Like most things from Brooklyn, the blackout cake doesn't give a damn what you think. Yeah, it's made from the darkest cocoa you can possibly imagine, so what? No, that's not buttercream, it's basically chocolate custard, smeared all over each layer of sponge cake. Got something to say about it? And, yeah, you do have to bake an entire extra layer of cake just to crumble it up and sprinkle it all over the glossy exterior... gotta problem? No? Good! Because all of these things result in literally the most perfect chocolate cake (vegan or otherwise) you've ever tasted.

To make the custard, place all the ingredients in a medium saucepan and whisk together well. Place over medium-low heat, whisking constantly, until the mixture has thickened to a dense custard, around 5 minutes.

Transfer the custard to a deep baking pan and cover with plastic wrap, so it is touching the surface. Leave to cool to room temperature before transferring to the fridge to chill for at least 4 hours, ideally overnight.

For the cake, butter 2 8in (20cm) springform cake pans and line them with parchment paper. Preheat the oven to 325°F (165°C) convection.

Place the melted vegan butter, vegetable oil, soy milk, vinegar, espresso powder, vanilla extract, and psyllium husk powder in a blender and blend until smooth.

Transfer the blended mixture to a bowl and add the light brown sugar and boiling water. Whisk until smooth, then set aside.

In a separate bowl, sift together the flour, baking soda, baking powder, cocoa powder, and ½ teaspoon salt. Add the wet ingredients to the dry and mix together gently, but do not overmix.

Divide the batter evenly between the 2 prepared pans and bake for 30–35 minutes, or until a skewer inserted in the center of the cakes comes out clean.

Place the cakes on a wire rack to cool for 15 minutes before removing from the pans, allowing the cakes to cool completely.

Once cooled, carefully slice both cakes in half horizontally, creating 4 layers. Choose the most irregular layer and break it up into even-size crumbs in a bowl. Set aside.

⇨

Sweet Stuff

Level ① ③

Blackout Cake

Choose the bottom layer of cake (the least attractive one is the contender here, unlike most things in life) and place on a serving plate.

Remove the chocolate custard from the fridge and remove the plastic wrap. Transfer the custard to a bowl and whisk until smooth. Spoon one-quarter of it onto the first cake and spread it out into an even layer.

Top with the second cake and repeat with a second layer of custard. Top with the final layer of cake. Transfer the cake and remaining custard to the fridge to chill for 10–20 minutes.

Spoon or pipe the remaining custard on the top and sides of the cake and spread into an even layer. Sprinkle the cake crumbs on the top of the cake and press carefully onto the top and sides.

Transfer the cake to the fridge to chill for at least 2 hours, or ideally overnight. As it chills, it'll become more fudgey. Slice and serve chilled, straight from the fridge.

Doughnut Peach Doughnuts

Makes 6–7

For the jam

21oz (600g) ripe peaches, pitted and finely chopped (around 8 doughnut peaches or 6 regular peaches)

1 lemon

2 cups (400g) granulated sugar

1 teaspoon vanilla bean paste

For the doughnuts

7 tablespoons lukewarm soy milk

2 tablespoons superfine sugar

2 teaspoons easy bake yeast

1¼ cups (160g) white bread flour

⅔ cup (70g) all-purpose flour, plus more to dust

2 tablespoons Vegan Butter (see page 272), or store-bought vegan butter, melted

6 tablespoons aquafaba

Vegetable oil, for deep-frying

¾ cup (150g) granulated sugar

Fine sea salt

Equipment needed

Meat or candy thermometer

These are doughnuts inspired by peaches, named after doughnuts... get into it! Around early May each year, I reconfigure the sensors in my nose to sniff out doughnut peaches wherever I am. They're simply my favorite fruit of all time. When the season's nearly over, I go into hibernation prep and make batches of doughnut peach jam, which is perfect for spreading on toast, or piping into doughnuts! For this recipe, try to get hold of a peach variety with yellow flesh rather than white. They're slightly less sweet, which really helps them to stay punchy when cooked.

Start with the jam. Place the peaches in a medium saucepan. Use a potato peeler to remove the zest of the lemon and add it to the peaches. Squeeze in the juice from the lemon, then add the sugar.

Place over medium-low heat and stir to combine. Bring to a simmer and allow to bubble for at least 10–15 minutes, stirring occasionally. The peaches should turn jammy and translucent.

It is ready when it reaches 215°F (105°C) on a thermometer. Stir in the vanilla bean paste, then remove from the heat and set aside to cool completely. While it cools, make the doughnuts.

In a small bowl, combine the lukewarm soy milk, 1 tablespoon of the superfine sugar, and the yeast. Whisk well and set aside for the yeast to activate (5–10 minutes).

In the bowl of a stand mixer fitted with the dough hook attachment, add the flours and remaining superfine sugar with ½ teaspoon salt. Mix briefly to combine.

Add the soy milk mixture to the flour along with the melted vegan butter and aquafaba. Knead on medium speed for about 5 minutes, or until a smooth and springy dough forms. Remove the bowl from the stand mixer and cover with a damp dish towel. Leave to rise for about 1½ hours, or until doubled in size.

Turn the dough onto a lightly floured work surface and press out the large air bubbles with your fingers. Give it a quick knead and then roll it out into a ⅝in- (1.5cm-) thick rectangle. Using a cookie cutter with a diameter of around 3in (7.5cm), cut out as many circles of dough as possible. Roll out and repeat with any excess dough. You should get a total of 6–7 doughnuts.

Place the cut doughnuts on individual squares of parchment paper, then place them all on a baking sheet. Cover again and let proof for 1 hour more.

Sweet Stuff Level ①②

Doughnut Peach Doughnuts

For frying and coating

Vegetable oil, for
  deep-frying
¾ cup (150g) granulated
  sugar

Equipment needed

Meat or candy thermometer
  (optional)

Fill a deep saucepan with 3in (7.5cm) vegetable oil. Place over medium-low heat and bring to 350°F (180°C). If you don't have a thermometer, you can test the oil with a scrap of excess dough: it should start bubbling immediately on contact with the oil and brown in around 30 seconds on each side.

When your oil is hot, carefully lower a doughnut into the fat, using the parchment paper to lift it. Use tongs to remove the paper once in the hot oil.

Allow to fry for 1 minute before checking the underside using a slotted spoon. If it's golden brown, flip the doughnut and repeat on the other side.

Remove the doughnut from the oil and place on 2 layers of paper towel. Repeat to fry the remaining doughnuts.

Place the granulated sugar in a small bowl and dunk each of the doughnuts to coat on both sides, then set aside.

Whisk the cooled peach jam to loosen it up, then transfer to a piping bag.

Pierce the bottom of a doughnut with a skewer and insert the tip of the piping bag. Gently squeeze the bag until the doughnut feels filled. Repeat with all the doughnuts, then serve.

Sweet Stuff

Level ①②③

Tres Leches Cake

Photographed on page 207

☺ x 8

For the cake

9oz (250ml) vegetable oil, plus more for the pan

3 cups (350g) all-purpose flour, plus more to dust

1 lemon wedge

7 tablespoons chilled aquafaba

¼ teaspoon cream of tartar

1⅔ cups (325g) superfine sugar, plus 2 tablespoons

1½ teaspoons baking powder

1 teaspoon baking soda

7oz (200ml) soy milk

1 teaspoon rice vinegar, or lemon juice

2 teaspoons vanilla bean paste, or vanilla extract

1½ teaspoons psyllium husk powder

Fine sea salt

For the milk mixture

1½ cups (350ml) full-fat plant milk (ideally oat or soy)

1½ cups (350ml) evaporated coconut milk

1⅓ cups (320ml) sweetened condensed coconut milk

3 tablespoons dark rum

1 tablespoon vanilla bean paste

This is probably my most requested dessert on Instagram: the Mexican classic. It's traditionally made with condensed milk, evaporated milk, and heavy cream, which seems like a lot of dairy for a dairy-free dessert! But don't worry, I've switched a few things up. We've got condensed coconut milk, evaporated coconut milk, and you'll even be making your own vegan whipped cream *from scratch*. FYI, that whipped cream is also ideal for scones, trifles, and desserts of all kinds.

Preheat the oven to 325°F (170°C) convection. Oil a deep 13 x 9 ½in (32 x 24cm) cake pan and dust with flour.

Use the lemon wedge to wipe the very clean bowl and whisk attachment of a stand mixer. Put the chilled aquafaba into the bowl and beat on high speed for a minimum of 3 minutes, or until soft peaks form. Add the cream of tartar and beat again to combine.

With the mixer still running, add the sugar little by little, and beat again until smooth and glossy. Set aside.

In a bowl, sift and stir together the flour, baking powder, baking soda, and ½ teaspoon salt.

Place the 2 tablespoons sugar, soy milk, rice vinegar or lemon juice, vanilla bean paste, vegetable oil, and psyllium husk powder in a blender. Blend until very smooth and thick.

Fold the blended soy milk mixture into the whipped aquafaba in 3 batches, folding very gently between additions.

Add the dry ingredients a few spoonfuls at a time, folding gently until just combined.

Carefully pour the batter into the prepared pan and bake for 35–40 minutes, or until risen and golden brown on top. Remove from the oven and leave to cool fully on a wire rack.

Once the cake has cooled, combine the milk mixture ingredients in a bowl and whisk well until completely combined and smooth. Pour half the milk mixture over the cooled cake (reserving the other half for serving), then cover and place in the fridge overnight.

Sweet Stuff

Level ① ② ③

Tres Leches Cake

For the whipped topping

1 cup (240ml) lukewarm soy milk

7oz (200ml) refined coconut oil, just melted but not hot

⅓ cup (40g) confectioners' sugar

2 teaspoons vanilla extract

Equipment needed

High-speed blender

<u>I have a huge bag of psyllium husk powder and I don't know what to do with it!</u>
Psyllium husk powder is made from superfinely ground psyllium seeds and is often used to replace gluten in gluten-free recipes, as well as for a dietary aid, since it's so high in fiber. A few years ago I found it works as an amazing egg replacement too: just blend it into your wet ingredients and it'll help to bind the batter and guarantee a light, springy sponge cake. If you can't get hold of it, ground flaxseed works well, too, but you'll need to double the quantity as they're about half as effective.

For the whipped topping, place the soy milk in the bowl of a high-speed blender, followed by the melted coconut oil. Blend together on the highest speed until smooth, then place in the fridge to chill overnight, ideally in an airtight container. At the same time, place the bowl of a stand mixer, or a medium mixing bowl, in the fridge to chill, too.

When you're ready to serve, transfer the cream to the chilled bowl of the stand mixer fitted with the whisk attachment. Or transfer to the chilled mixing bowl and use a handheld electric mixer. Starting on a low speed, work your way up gradually toward the highest setting of the beaters, whipping the cream until its texture has thickened and it falls from the whisk in ribbons.

Add the confectioners' sugar and vanilla extract, then whisk again on high speed until soft peaks form. Be careful not to overbeat the cream, or it will split.

Top the cake with the whipped cream, piping it on if you want to be fancy.

Serve immediately, or keep in the fridge for up to 3 days before slicing and serving with the remaining milk mixture.

Nanny Sadie's Vanilla Custard Slice

Makes 8

2 x 13oz (370g) package ready-rolled vegan puff pastry

4 cups (1 liter) soy milk, plus 2 tablespoons

1½ tablespoons vanilla bean paste (or the seeds from 1 vanilla pod)

1¼ cups (250g) superfine sugar

2 x 13½oz (400ml) cans coconut milk

1 cup (120g) cornstarch

⅓ cup (90g) Vegan Butter (see page 272), or store-bought vegan butter, chopped

2⅔ cups (260g) confectioners' sugar

As a kid, Nanny Sadie's house was my destination for sick days when both my parents were out at work. We'd play card games, read each other's tea leaves, and eat way too many pastries from the local Sayers bakery. No wonder I was always pulling sickies! Nanny's favorite was always the custard slice, so, naturally, she'd get two, so we didn't have to share.

Preheat the oven to 350°F (180°C) convection and line a large baking sheet with parchment paper. Unroll 1 sheet of puff pastry onto the lined baking sheet and top with another layer of parchment paper. Top with a second baking sheet.

Repeat this process with the second sheet of puff pastry, or if you're short on baking sheets, bake the pastry 1 sheet at a time.

Place in the preheated oven to bake for 25 minutes. Remove from the oven and lift off the top baking sheets to allow the pastry to cool fully. Once cooled, trim the baked pastry sheets to fit inside a 9in (23cm) square cake pan. Place 1 sheet inside the pan.

Place the 4 cups (1 liter) soy milk, vanilla, superfine sugar, coconut milk, and cornstarch in a large saucepan. Place over medium-low heat and whisk constantly until very thick. If the custard is not thick after 8–10 minutes, increase the heat slightly and persevere!

Once the custard is thick, remove the saucepan from the heat and add the vegan butter. Stir well with a spatula until the butter is melted and evenly distributed.

Immediately pour the custard into the baking pan with the sheet of puff pastry at the bottom. Top with the second sheet of pastry and leave to cool on the work surface for 10 minutes.

Transfer to the fridge and leave to set for at least 6 hours.

Once cooled and set, mix the confectioners' sugar and 2 tablespoons soy milk together in a bowl. Pour the icing over the top of the custard slice and spread into a thin layer. You could even try your hand at feathering the icing into patterns with a touch of chocolate at this stage, if you like. Return to the fridge for 10 minutes more to set before slicing and serving.

Manchester Tart

☺ × 8

11½oz (320g) ready-rolled
vegan pie dough
4oz (120g) seedless
raspberry jam
2 bananas, peeled
9oz (250ml) soy milk
7oz (200ml) canned coconut
milk
1 tablespoon cornstarch
4 tablespoons vegan
custard powder
2 teaspoons vanilla extract
¼ cup (50g) sugar
3½oz (100g) unsweetened,
dried coconut

Equipment needed
Baking beans (optional)

I don't care what you say, Manchester tart is a certified queer icon. Just try to tell me that the person who first stuck raspberry jam, custard, and coconut in a tart wasn't an LGBTQ+ hero before their time! In a world of traditional, boring custard tarts, it's bravely flamboyant and I identified with it from the second I first tried it in primary school. Not to mention it's insanely delicious.

Preheat the oven to 400°F (200°C) convection and put on a baking sheet.

Line a 9in (23cm) pie pan with the pie dough and prick the bottom with a fork. Trim off the excess dough, then line with parchment paper and fill with baking beans. If you don't have baking beans, raw rice or dried chickpeas work well.

Place on the hot baking sheet in the oven and bake for 20 minutes. Remove from the oven and remove the baking beans and parchment paper, then return to the oven for 5–8 minutes, or until just crisp but not overly browned. Transfer to a wire rack to cool.

Once cooled, spread the bottom of the tart case with the jam. Now slice the bananas into ¼in- (7mm-) thick coins and arrange evenly over the jam.

Now, make the custard. Place the soy milk, coconut milk, cornstarch, custard powder, vanilla extract, and sugar into a medium pan. Place over medium heat and whisk constantly until the mixture begins to steam. Reduce the heat to low and continue whisking until the custard has thickened up dramatically.

Pour the thickened custard over the bananas in the tart crust and spread into a smooth layer with a knife. Sprinkle with the coconut and set aside to cool to room temperature.

Transfer to the fridge to chill and set for 20–30 minutes before slicing and serving.

Sweet Stuff

Level ① ② ⑳

Lemon Poppy Seed Muffins

Makes 12

½ cup (120ml) soy milk, at room temperature
2 tablespoons lemon juice
1 teaspoon lemon extract
¼ cup (65ml) water
5 tablespoons vegetable oil
1½ teaspoon psyllium husk powder
2¾ cups (320g) all-purpose flour
2½ teaspoons baking powder
1 cup (200g) granulated sugar
Finely grated zest of 1 large lemon
5 tablespoons Vegan Butter (see page 272), or store-bought vegan butter, at room temperature
2 tablespoons poppy seeds, plus 1 teaspoon
2 tablespoons demerara sugar
Fine sea salt

For the glaze
⅔ cup (80g) confectioners' sugar
2 tablespoons lemon juice

I'm so glad we've all agreed that cupcakes are over and muffins can return to their rightful spot as The Best Baked Thing In Little Paper Liners. Muffins feel like a bit of an actual meal, and I want to thank them personally for being so substantial and filling. The key to a crumbly muffin top is to make sure you don't overwork the batter, so keep the stirring to a minimum.

Preheat the oven to 350°F (180°C) convection and line a 12-hole muffin tray pan with paper liners.

In the bowl of a blender, combine the soy milk, lemon juice, lemon extract, water, vegetable oil, and psyllium husk powder. Blend until smooth and set aside. Alternatively, place the ingredients in a tall container and blend with an immersion blender until very smooth.

In a bowl, sift together the flour, baking powder, and ½ teaspoon salt. Stir together until well combined and set aside.

If using a stand mixer, remove the bowl and combine the granulated sugar and lemon zest. Use your fingers to rub them together until fragrant. If using a handheld electric mixer, follow this step in a bowl.

Return the bowl to the stand mixer, if using, and attach the paddle attachment. Add the butter and beat on medium speed until light and creamy, around 2 minutes. Alternatively, cream the butter and sugar together using a handheld electric mixer.

Add half the soy milk mixture to the butter mixture and beat to combine. Now add half the flour mixture and beat on low speed until just combined. Repeat the process with the second half of the soy milk mixture, followed by the remaining flour mixture. Finally, add the 2 tablespoons poppy seeds and mix until just combined.

Divide the mix between the 12 paper liners and sprinkle the tops with the demerara sugar. Bake for 25–30 minutes, until risen and golden brown. Once baked, remove from the oven and place the muffin pan on a wire rack. Allow to cool completely before removing the muffins from the pan.

Once the muffins are at room temperature, sift the confectioners' sugar into a bowl. Add the lemon juice and whisk together well until smooth. Drizzle the glaze over the muffins and sprinkle with the 1 teaspoon poppy seeds. Leave to set for 15 minutes, then serve.

Spotted Dick and Custard

Makes 4

For the puddings

⅞ cup (150g) currants (or raisins)

¾ cup (175ml) water

Vegan Butter (see page 272), or store-bought vegan butter, for the basins

1¾ cups (200g) self-rising flour

⅓ cup (80g) superfine sugar

5⅕ tablespoons shredded vegetable suet

Finely grated zest 1 lemon

⅔ cup (150g) soy milk

Fine sea salt

For the custard

1¼ cups (300ml) soy milk

13½oz (400ml) can coconut milk

⅓ cup (40g) cornstarch

2 teaspoons vanilla bean paste

¾ cups (150g) superfine sugar

Nothing hits that nostalgia button for any Brit over the age of thirty like spotted dick. This old school–lunch classic is the edible equivalent of spelling 80085 on a calculator: feels a bit cheeky still, even though I'm thirty-five. But, I assure you, this steamed pudding holds its own and was surprisingly easy to veganize. Vegetable suet and soy milk do the job perfectly; the proof is in the pudding!

To make the puddings, place the currants and water in a small saucepan and place over medium-low heat. Simmer for 5 minutes, then remove from the heat.

Butter 4 nonstick individual pudding basins. Set aside.

Fill a saucepan halfway with water and place over medium heat. Once boiling, top the saucepan with a steamer basket. Alternatively, fill and switch on an electric steamer.

In a bowl, mix the flour, sugar, suet, and lemon zest with a pinch of salt. Add the soy milk and mix until just combined. Drain the currants and gently stir them in.

Divide the batter among the prepared basins, leaving a little room at the top of each for the pudding to expand. Wrap each basin completely in foil and place in the steamer.

Steam for 1 hour. When the puddings have 10 minutes left to steam, make the custard.

In a medium saucepan, whisk together the soy milk, coconut milk, cornstarch, vanilla bean paste, and superfine sugar.

Place over medium-low heat and whisk constantly until the custard has thickened.

Remove the puddings from the steamer and leave to sit for 5 minutes before unwrapping the foil. Turn out onto a plate and top with custard before serving.

Chocolate and Caramel Crêpe Cake

☺ x 8–12

Is it a normal-size cake made from loads of superthin crêpes, or is it a massive cake made from dozens of huge sponge cakes, photographed from really far away? There's only one way to find out: follow this recipe! Ah, well, the title kind of gives it away, too...

For the caramel

1½oz (45g) raw unsalted cashews, or sunflower seeds

⅓ cup (80ml) cold water

⅓ cup (100g) coconut cream (the solid white stuff at the top of a can of chilled coconut milk)

1 cup (200g) superfine sugar

½ teaspoon vanilla bean paste

Sea salt flakes

For the crêpes

6 cups (675g) all-purpose flour

5½ cups (1.3 liters) soy milk

6 tablespoons vegetable oil, plus more for frying

3 tablespoons superfine sugar

1 teaspoon vanilla extract

To make the caramel, place the cashews in a medium heatproof bowl and cover with boiling water. Cover with a plate and leave to soak for 30 minutes.

Once soaked, drain the cashews and transfer to a high-speed blender with the cold water. Blend until very smooth. Once smooth, add the coconut cream and pulse-blend until combined and smooth.

In a medium, high-sided saucepan over medium-low heat, add the sugar. Stirring constantly, heat until the sugar is completely melted and is turning a nice golden brown (don't worry if it smokes slightly).

Remove from the heat and add the coconut cashew cream mixture. The caramel will splutter and spit, so be careful. Stir gently until combined, then add the vanilla and a pinch of salt. Stir well.

Return to low heat and simmer gently for a minute or 2. Remove from the heat and set aside to cool to room temperature. Once cool, place the mixture in the fridge to chill for 1 hour.

Meanwhile, make the crêpes. In a large bowl, combine all the ingredients and whisk until smooth. Set aside for 10 minutes.

Heat a medium, nonstick frying pan (or ideally a crêpe pan) over medium heat and drizzle with a little vegetable oil.

Use a ladle to scoop up a scant ½ cup (100ml) of batter and pour into the center of the hot pan. Swirl the pan around to make a large thin crêpe that touches the edges of the pan. Cook until the top of the crêpe looks matte and no longer wet.

Flip the crêpe and fry for 1 minute more, or until lightly browned underneath. Remove from the pan and set aside on a baking sheet to cool. Repeat with exactly the same amount of batter, making sure the crêpe is the same size as the first one. Continue until no batter remains: you should end up with about 20 crêpes.

Place the cooked crêpes in the fridge to chill.

Chocolate and Caramel Crêpe Cake

Equipment needed

High-speed blender

For the buttercream

4oz (110g) vegan dark chocolate, at least 70 percent cacao, broken up

7 tablespoons Vegan Butter (see page 272), or store-bought vegan butter, at room temperature

7 tablespoons (100g) vegan margarine, at room temperature

¼ cup (20g) cocoa powder

2¾ cups (315g) confectioners' sugar

Meanwhile, make the buttercream. Carefully melt the dark chocolate in short bursts in the microwave, stirring regularly to ensure it doesn't burn. Or melt it in a heatproof bowl set over a pan of simmering water, making sure the bowl does not touch the water. Set aside and allow to cool for 10 minutes.

In the bowl of a stand mixer fitted with the whisk attachment, or using a handheld electric mixer, combine the vegan butter and margarine. Whisk on high-speed until smooth and fluffy (about 3 minutes).

Add the cocoa powder and beat on low speed until completely smooth. Add the confectioners' sugar a spoonful at a time, beating between additions.

Add the melted, cooled chocolate and beat a final time for 2 minutes, or until the buttercream is very smooth and fluffy.

Place a crêpe in the center of a serving plate or cake stand and top with around 2 tablespoons of buttercream. Spread the buttercream right to the edges of the crêpe in a thin layer. Repeat with the next crêpe, layering crêpes and buttercream until you have stacked all the crêpes in a neat cylinder.

Top the final crêpe with a generous layer of buttercream. Remove the caramel from the fridge and drizzle half over the top layer of buttercream. Slice and serve the cake with the remaining caramel sauce.

Ice Cream Party

Professionally speaking, ice cream was my gateway to the food world, so I couldn't write this book without a vegan version. In fact, here are three: knock yourself out! I've tried to keep things simple in terms of flavors, but you will definitely need an ice-cream machine to get decent results. Just a cheap one with a freezer bowl will do; nothing fancy is needed, unless you're feeling bougie, in which case I recommend eating your ice cream with a gold teaspoon. My favorite is the latte ice cream on page 200, which features the wonder that nearly broke the internet: dalgona whip! It's a strange, light, fluffy miracle that happens when you whip water, instant coffee, and sugar together, and it makes an irresistibly creamy topping for any cup of coffee as well as for vegan ice cream.

Vanilla Ice Cream

Photographed on page 222

Makes
2½ cups (600ml)

7oz (200ml) soy milk

7oz (200ml) canned coconut milk

⅓ cup (80g) refined coconut oil, melted

⅔ cup (120g) superfine sugar

2 teaspoons sunflower lecithin

3 teaspoons vanilla bean paste

Equipment needed
High-speed blender
Ice cream machine

Place a 1-quart (1-liter) freezer-proof container in the freezer to chill.

Place all the ingredients in the bowl of a high-speed blender and blend until completely smooth. For maximum flavor, cover with a lid and set aside to allow the vanilla to infuse for at least 1 hour.

Blend again, once infused, until smooth and then transfer to an ice-cream machine and churn according to the manufacturer's instructions.

Transfer from the machine to the chilled container and place in the freezer to hard-freeze for at least 5 hours, or ideally overnight, before serving.

Sweet Stuff

Level ① ② ③

Dalgona Latte
Ice Cream

Makes
2 ½ cups (600ml)

For the ice cream
7oz (200ml) oat milk
7oz (200ml) canned
	coconut milk
⅓ cup (80g) refined
	coconut oil, melted
⅔ cup (120g)
	superfine sugar
2 teaspoons
	sunflower lecithin
2 tablespoons vanilla
	bean paste
2 tablespoons instant
	espresso powder

For the dalgona whip
3 tablespoons instant coffee
3 tablespoons
	superfine sugar
3 tablespoons boiling water

Equipment needed
High-speed blender
Ice cream machine

Place a 1-quart (1-liter) freezer-proof container in the freezer to chill.

Place all the ingredients for the ice cream, except the instant espresso powder, in the bowl of a high-speed blender and blend until completely smooth. For maximum flavor, cover with a lid and set aside to allow the vanilla to infuse for at least 1 hour.

Blend again, once infused, until smooth, then transfer half of the mix to an ice-cream machine and churn according to the manufacturer's instructions. Add the instant espresso powder to the remaining half of the ice-cream mix and blend again until smooth.

Transfer the frozen ice cream from the machine to the chilled container and place in the freezer. Meanwhile, churn the remaining coffee-flavored half of the ice-cream mix according to the manufacturer's instructions.

Swirl the coffee ice cream through the vanilla ice cream in the container, cover, and return to the freezer to hard-freeze for at least 5 hours, or ideally overnight, before serving.

To make the dalgona whip, place all the ingredients in the bowl of a stand mixer fitted with the whisk attachment and beat on high speed until stiff peaks form. If stored in the fridge, the dalgona whip should stay whipped for an hour or so, but it's best not to make it too far in advance. Spoon the whip onto the ice cream before serving.

Sweet Stuff

Level ① ② ③

Raspberry Ripple Ice Cream

Photographed on page 222

Makes
2 ½ cups (600ml)

For the ripple

7oz (200g)
    frozen raspberries

⅔ cup (120g)
    superfine sugar

For the ice cream

7oz (200ml) full-fat oat milk

7oz (200ml) canned full-fat
    coconut milk

⅓ cup (80g) refined
    coconut oil, melted

⅔ cup (120g) superfine
    sugar

2 teaspoons sunflower
    lecithin

2 tablespoons vanilla
    bean paste

Equipment needed

High-speed blender

Ice cream machine

To make the ripple, place the raspberries and sugar in a medium saucepan and place over medium heat. Stirring constantly, cook until all the sugar has dissolved and the raspberries have given up their juice. Reduce the heat to low.

Cook until the raspberries have just about lost their shape (about 5 minutes). Remove from the heat and pass the syrup through a sieve to remove the seeds and pulp. Use the back of a spoon to carefully push all the syrup through. Cover and set aside to cool to room temperature before transferring to the fridge.

Place a 1-quart (1-liter) freezerproof container in the freezer to chill.

Place all the ice-cream ingredients in the bowl of a high-speed blender and blend until completely smooth. For maximum flavor, cover with a lid and set aside to allow the vanilla to infuse for at least 1 hour.

Blend again, once infused, until smooth and then transfer to an ice-cream machine and churn according to the manufacturer's instructions.

Working quickly, transfer a few spoonfuls of soft-frozen ice cream from the machine into the prepared frozen container. Drizzle a little of the chilled raspberry ripple syrup on top. Follow with a few more spoons of the ice cream, repeating the process until you have layered and rippled ice cream and raspberry syrup.

Transfer to the freezer to hard-freeze for at least 5 hours, or ideally overnight, before serving.

Sweet Stuff

Level ① ② ⑶

Veganetta

🙂 x 10

2 x 14oz (400ml) cans
    coconut milk,
    refrigerated for 24 hours
7oz (200ml) can sweetened
    condensed coconut milk
1¼ cups (250g)
    superfine sugar
2 teaspoons vanilla bean
    paste, or vanilla extract
1¾oz (50g) dark chocolate,
    at least 70 percent cacao,
    broken into pieces
1 tablespoon refined
    coconut oil
2 tablespoons
    slivered almonds

When I was a kid, Viennetta was a once-a-year treat. When researching this recipe, I asked Mam why we didn't eat Viennetta more often and her response was, "Who do you think I am? The Queen?" To this day, my family considers it dessert royalty and I've pined for it ever since I went vegan. BUT, NO LONGER! My take on the aspirational retro classic ice-cream cake uses just seven ingredients and requires no churning and no cooking! I guarantee the results will make you feel like an upwardly mobile young veganetta go-getter!

Open the 2 cans refrigerated coconut milk, scoop off the solidified coconut cream, and place in a large bowl, or the bowl of a stand mixer. (You won't need the remaining coconut water in the cans, but reserve it for making cocktails or smoothies.)

Line a loaf pan (any size will do) with parchment paper and place in the freezer to chill.

Whip the coconut cream on high speed using a handheld electric mixer, or the whisk attachment of a stand mixer, until it has increased in volume and is light and fluffy like whipped cream.

In a separate bowl, mix together the coconut milk, sugar, and vanilla. Add it to the whipped coconut cream in 4 additions, beating gently between each.

Transfer one-quarter of the mixture to a piping bag. Place the chocolate and the coconut oil in a microwaveable bowl and place in the microwave on full power for 15 seconds. Stir well and repeat twice more until the mixture is melted and glossy. Transfer to a second piping bag.

Remove the loaf pan from the freezer and pipe in a layer of the coconut cream mixture; you can pipe in wavy zigzags or straight lines, it's up to you! Top this layer with a thin drizzle of the dark chocolate and place the pan back in the freezer for 5 minutes, or until the chooolate has set. Repeat this process, refilling the piping bag with the next quarter of the coconut cream mixture as needed. Once you've run out of coconut cream mixture, top with a final drizzle of the dark chocolate, and sprinkle with the slivered almonds.

Freeze for a minimum of 6 hours before slicing and serving.

Building Block Recipes

"Stuffed full of tips and techniques to transform you into a versatile, adaptive vegan cook who can blast out a banquet without a recipe in a matter of minutes!"

My dream for this book has always been to create more than just a collection of fun recipes and gorgeous pictures. Sure, I wanted to write and photograph a really sexy page-turner, but also to make something actually useful for new and old vegans alike. In my mind, this book should sit somewhere in the middle of the handbook/manifesto/cookbook Venn diagram. So, in addition to a bunch of kick-ass recipes, this book is stuffed full of tips and techniques to transform you into a versatile, adaptive vegan cook who can blast out a banquet without a recipe in a matter of minutes!

The building block recipes in this chapter are the stuff you need to know to *really* get cracking in the kitchen. Over the past six years, I've made a log of my methods for making meat substitutes, plant-based cheeses, and essential sauces, and now is my time to pass it on to you, just like Yoda teaching Luke the ways of The Force. Nah, don't mention it! Just buy me a pack of chips and a can of fizzy soda to say thank you.

I refer to the recipes here a lot as elements of other dishes in this book, but I urge you to make these meats, cheeses, and sauces and use them however you wish. Part of the joy of vegan cooking is that it encourages you to cook creatively, since you can't just grab all your old favorite ingredients. A good place to start is to think about a meal you crave since going vegan (or a meal you think you would crave, if you haven't made the switch yet), then figure out what's missing. Are you craving pasta bake with bubbly golden melted cheese? Then put my vegan mozzarella to good use! Is it smoky bacon you're dreaming of? Then get creative with my paper tofu bacon recipe! Now's your chance to go rogue and have some fun!

Meats

You probably weren't expecting a section entitled Meats in your vegan cookbook, so let me explain briefly... I was a kid when I first became vegetarian around thirty years ago, so my memories of meat are few and far between. A rare Happy Meal in the back of our broken-down Nissan Micra, spaghetti and meatballs at a sleepover, and hotdogs in the Ikea café are essentially the highlights reel. But I believe there's something intensely and irreversibly formative about all those early food memories, no matter how hazy (and meaty) they are. Those are the memories, in a lot of ways, that are responsible for how I feel about food. The way a roast dinner feels comforting, or spicy tacos feel exciting. The way a particular stew might feel like home, or ham sandwiches might feel like a party at Aunty Lilly's house.

Although I decided to stop eating meat a long time ago, I couldn't part with those feelings and memories if I tried; they're part of my food culture and, in turn, part of my identity. Refusing to cook these nostalgic, evocative dishes just because I no longer eat meat feels a lot like throwing the pasta out with the pasta water: what a waste! Learning to make insanely tasty meat substitutes unlocks all those old recipes and expands the possibilities of vegan cooking. If you still feel like meat substitutes aren't for you, no biggie, just skip this section. But if you're into it (like I am), here are some tips and recipes for making meatless magic happen in your kitchen!

Seitan Worship

Seitan is a super-old Chinese method of making protein-rich meat substitutes, from wheat. It's also my favorite solution to replacing meat. Some methods require you to wash flour until a dough forms, then keep washing until only gluten (wheat protein) remains, but this process takes ages and isn't quite as therapeutic as TikTok would have you believe. I recommend using store-bought wheat gluten instead and having a nice cup of tea with all your spare time.

Pick Your Wet Ingredients
To make a seitan dough, you'll need to hydrate wheat gluten. This is your first chance to get some big flavor involved, so don't blow it! Use stuff like veggie stock, soy sauce, and liquid smoke. It's good to try to involve lots of protein at this stage, too, as it keeps the seitan meaty, which is why I blend up tofu and cans of cannellini beans for the recipes in the pages that follow.

Knead or Blend Together
Next, you'll need to get messy! Mix together wet ingredients and wheat gluten until a dough forms, then knead like your life depends on it!

Building Block Recipes:
Meats

Building Block Recipes:
Meats

For extra-stringy, fibrous seitan, I like to use a blender for this kneading process. It ensures all the strands of gluten are aligned and results in a super-smooth dough.

Wrap the Dough
As it cooks, seitan will want to expand, like bread. Your job is to deny it of this very desire, unless you want soft, spongy seitan rather than meaty, firm seitan. I tend to wrap my dough first in parchment paper, muslin, or cheesecloth to stop it from expanding. Chef's twine is helpful here, too, particularly for larger portions of seitan.

Cook the Dough
Cooking the dough "sets" the texture and shape of the seitan, so this is where you get to decide what the meat will look like. Take this into account when wrapping your dough. For instance, if you're making my Seitan Chicken (see page 235), you may want to shape the dough into fillets to look like chicken breasts. You'll then steam, boil, or roast the dough until firm. If you choose to boil it, this is another shot to get lots of flavor into the seitan, so don't use plain water. Make a super-flavorful broth instead and your seitan will be next level.

Marinate or Cook Again!
Your seitan is now technically ready to eat, or cook and add to a dish, but you can also dial things up a notch at this final stage. This is a great time to marinate the seitan and let it soak up some more big flavors! Cover the seitan with the cooled poaching broth, or baste it in the sauce you plan to cook it with. A good twenty-four hours in the fridge should do it. Alternatively, you're ready to slice, dice, and cook up a meaty storm (obviously, without the meat).

Building Block Recipes:
Meats

Seitan Chicken

Makes 8

For the poaching broth

5 quarts (5 liters) water
1 garlic bulb, halved
1 onion, halved
1 carrot, chopped into
    1in (2.5cm) chunks
2 celery ribs, chopped into
    1in (2.5cm) chunks
4 tablespoons white
    miso paste
½ cup (120ml) vegan dry
    white wine (optional)
2 tablespoons sugar
2 tablespoons massel
    chicken stock powder,
    or vegan mushroom
    bouillon powder
4 bay leaves
1 teaspoon black
    peppercorns
Fine sea salt

For the seitan

10½oz (300g) pack
    silken tofu
14oz (400g) can cannellini
    beans, including the liquid
2 tablespoons white
    miso paste
2 teaspoons rice vinegar,
    or apple cider vinegar,
    or white wine vinegar
2 tablespoons massel
    chicken stock powder,
    or vegan mushroom
    bouillon powder
¼ cup (60ml) vegetable oil,
    or any neutral oil
3½ cups (400g) vital
    wheat gluten

Equipment needed

High-speed blender (optional)

A really great place to start with your seitan-making adventures is with vegan chicken. Are you excited at the prospect of literally being able to make your own chicken, and not in a weird God-playing, cloney-science, Dolly the Sheep way? You should be! You'll find this stuff in my Grandma's Chicken Saaalad, Sriracha Cashew Chicken, and, of course, Fancy Fried Chicken (see pages 89, 135, and 138), but I also want to encourage you to experiment with it. Why not baste some seitan chicken with my quick Gochujang Barbecue Sauce (see page 265) and stick it on the grill? Or shred it up and stuff yourself some chicken tinga tacos? Got overexcited and made too much (story of my life)? Just pop your seitan in a container, cover with the poaching broth, and freeze it.

Take a look at the process photographs on the previous page, to get a feel for the method that follows. For the broth, fill a large saucepan for which you have a lid with the water, place over high heat, and bring to a boil. Add all the poaching broth ingredients with 2 teaspoons salt, then reduce the heat to simmer, and cover with a lid.

To make the seitan, place all the ingredients, except the vital wheat gluten, into a high-speed blender with 2 teaspoons salt and blend until very smooth. If your blender isn't high speed, just get the mixture as smooth as possible. Place a fine-meshed sieve over a bowl and pour the mixture through.

Return the mixture to the blender, add the vital wheat gluten, and blend until smooth and very stretchy, 2–5 minutes. If your blender struggles, remove half, then blend the seitan in 2 batches. Stop the blender and leave the dough to rest for 10 minutes.

Blend again for 1 minute. At this stage, the seitan dough should be very stringy, almost the texture of chewing gum.

Remove the dough from the blender and knead lightly until it comes together. Divide it into 8 pieces, roughly 5 ½oz (155g) each. Roll the portions into balls, cover with an upturned roasting pan, and leave to rest for 10 minutes.

Meanwhile, cut out 3 ½ x 9in (8 x 22cm) squares of muslin or cheesecloth. Set aside.

Working with 1 portion of dough at a time, roll with the palms of your hands into a long snake, around 12in (30cm) in length. Don't worry if the dough tries to spring back slightly.

Hold both ends of the length of dough and twist in opposite directions until the dough feels taut (5–6 full rotations). With the dough still twisted, tie in 2 knots and squeeze gently until the knots hold.

Building Block Recipes: Meats

Level

Place the knotted portion of dough onto a square of muslin or cheesecloth. Tie opposing corners of the cloth so the dough is tightly wrapped. Set aside and repeat with the remaining pieces of dough and cloth.

Once all the pieces of dough are knotted and wrapped, carefully place them in the simmering broth, cover with a lid, and reduce the temperature to the lowest setting.

Simmer the seitan for 1 hour. The seitan will float to the top and expand in size, so be sure to stir every 10 minutes or so. Do not allow the broth to come to a rolling boil: it should simmer very gently. If most of the broth evaporates, add more freshly boiled water.

Once cooked, turn off the heat and leave the pan of seitan and broth to cool to room temperature.

When the broth is at room temperature, transfer to the fridge. Leave to chill and marinate for at least 4 hours, or ideally overnight. The seitan is now ready to eat or grill, fry, roast, or cook however you would cook chicken.

To store, place in an airtight container and cover with the remaining broth. Refrigerate for up to 1 week, or freeze for up to 1 month.

> **Recipe note**
> This seitan is made in a blender or food processor, which helps to keep it super-fibrous and meaty. If your blender can't handle the dough, don't worry. Just knead together by hand until you have a coarse dough, then divide into 2–4 and blend in these smaller portions until very stretchy and fibrous. In the image for this recipe I've served the seitan chicken on rice with cucumber, scallion, carrot, and toasted black-sesame seeds with sriracha sauce, but feel free to use however you would real chicken.

Building Block Recipes: Meats

Seitan Roast

Makes 1

For the seitan

10½oz (300g) pack silken tofu

7oz (200g) fresh raw beets, peeled and cubed

3 tablespoons vegetable oil

3 tablespoons English mustard

2 tablespoons massel beef stock powder, or vegan mushroom bouillon powder

1 tablespoon onion powder

2 tablespoons nutritional yeast

1 tablespoon rice, white wine, or apple cider vinegar

1 teaspoon black molasses

3 tablespoons dark soy sauce

3¾ cups (430g) vital wheat gluten

Fine sea salt

Equipment needed

High-speed blender (optional)

Vegan Agony Aunt

How do I make my seitan not-spongy?

Seitan turns out spongy when it's not wrapped tightly during the cooking process or when you've not kneaded the dough enough (or both). Be sure to give it a good few minutes of kneading or blending, then wrap tightly to stop it from expanding.

For a long time, the only beef I had was with my brother for dropping my Tamagotchi named Paul in the dog's water bowl. I miss you Paul, RIP. Now that I'm older and my therapist says I need to move on, I find my beef elsewhere. Enter my super-beefy seitan roast! Perfect for a dinner with the in-laws or a solo Sunday roast (with leftover butties the next day). Don't be daunted by all the ingredients, they're mostly just the same spices and seasonings you'd find on a traditional roast.

To make the seitan dough, place all the ingredients, except the vital wheat gluten, into a high-speed blender with 2 teaspoons salt and blend until very smooth. If your blender isn't high-speed, just get the mixture as smooth as possible. Place a fine-meshed sieve over a bowl and pour the mixture through.

Return the mixture to the blender and add the vital wheat gluten. Blend again until a smooth, very stretchy dough forms that's almost the texture of chewing gum (about 5 minutes). If your blender struggles to manage the dough, remove half and blend it in 2 batches.

Turn off the blender and leave the dough to rest for 10 minutes. Remove the dough from the blender, place on a work surface, and cover with an upturned bowl to prevent it from drying out.

For the roast, preheat the oven to 325°F (165°C) convection. Uncover the seitan dough and roll with the palms of your hands into an 8in (20cm) cylinder. Use a sharp knife to slice the dough lengthwise into 3, then pinch them together at one end. Braid the pieces together, stretching the dough where necessary. When you reach the end of the strands of dough, pinch them all together tightly. You should have a braid of dough around 8in (20cm) long.

Building Block Recipes: Meats

Level ① ② ③

Seitan Roast

For roasting

4 teaspoons black
    peppercorns
1 teaspoon mustard seeds
3 bay leaves
4 thyme sprigs
4 rosemary sprigs
1 tablespoon massel beef
    stock powder, or vegan
    mushroom bouillon powder
3 tablespoons dark soy sauce
2 teaspoons Marmite
2 tablespoons light
    brown sugar
1 garlic bulb, sliced in half
    across the middle
1 onion, quartered
1 carrot, quartered
2 celery ribs, quartered
4 cups (1 liter) boiling water,
    plus more if needed

Roughly crack the black peppercorns in a mortar and pestle, then spread out on a work surface. Roll the braid of dough in the peppercorns, ensuring all sides are coated.

Wrap the dough tightly in parchment paper, twisting the ends like a Christmas cracker. Wrap again in muslin or cheesecloth. Use chef's twine to tie up the seitan multiple times tightly along the length and around the circumference of the dough, like a joint of meat.

Place all the remaining roasting ingredients in a casserole dish with 1 teaspoon salt and stir to combine. Carefully lower the seitan roast in, making sure it's roughly half-covered with the broth (if not, add extra boiling water). Cover with a lid, then place in the oven to cook for 1 hour.

Remove the casserole dish from the oven and rotate the seitan joint so the opposite side is submerged in the broth. Top off the broth with boiling water to roughly halfway up the roast (if necessary), then return to the oven for 40 minutes more.

Remove from the oven and increase the oven temperature to 400°F (200°C) convection. Remove the seitan from the broth and cut off the chef's twine, cloth and parchment paper. Return the seitan to the casserole dish and use a pastry brush to baste the joint with the remaining broth, being careful not to brush off all the peppercorns. Return to the oven for 10–20 minutes, or until the outside of the seitan is browned. Baste the joint again with the broth before serving.

To store, wrap tightly in plastic wrap and refrigerate for up to 1 week, or freeze for up to 1 month.

Seitan Chorizo

Makes 8

1¾ cups (200g) vital wheat
gluten
1 tablespoon fennel seeds
½ teaspoon black
peppercorns
1 teaspoon onion powder
2 teaspoons garlic powder
2½ tablespoons smoked
paprika
1 teaspoon cayenne pepper
2 tablespoons olive oil
1 small red onion,
finely chopped
6 garlic cloves, chopped
3 sundried tomatoes, drained
3½oz (100g) jarred roasted
red peppers, drained
¼ cup (60g) tomato purée
3 tablespoons wholegrain
mustard
1½ tablespoons red
miso paste
2 tablespoons massel pork
stock powder, or vegan
mushroom bouillon powder
¾ cup (180ml) water
3 tablespoons ground TVP
Fine sea salt

Equipment needed
High-speed blender (optional)

> **Recipe note**
> Mustard obviously doesn't
> belong in traditional chorizo,
> but it acts as an emulsifier
> in this recipe and helps to
> hold everything together.
> If you'd like to try the recipe
> without the mustard,
> exchange it for 1 teaspoon
> psyllium husk powder
> instead but, personally, I
> love the extra kick.

What better way to kick off a summery stew or a punchy chili than by frying off some crumbly cubes of chorizo? What's cool though is that this recipe works equally well as a cold cut in sandwiches or on a cheeseboard. Live your true picnic nerd fantasy and pack a few slices, like jerky, for a snack on long drives and train trips, along with lots of ginger ale.

Place the vital wheat gluten in the bowl of a stand mixer fitted with the paddle attachment, or place in a large mixing bowl.

Place a medium saucepan over medium heat and add the fennel seeds. Toast the seeds for a minute or 2 until very fragrant. Transfer the fennel seeds to a spice grinder along with the remaining spices and 2 teaspoons salt. Grind to an even-ground spice blend. Alternatively, grind with a mortar and pestle, or in a high-speed blender. Set aside.

Place the saucepan back on the stove, this time over medium-low heat, and add the olive oil. Once hot, add the onion and fry until soft but not browned. Add the garlic and fry for a minute more.

Remove the onion and garlic from the heat and allow to cool on the work surface for 5 minutes. Transfer to a high-speed blender and add the spice blend and all remaining ingredients except the TVP. Purée the mixture completely. Add the puréed spicy paste to the vital wheat gluten and run the stand mixer on low speed for 8–10 minutes. If kneading by hand, mix everything together

until a coarse dough forms, then transfer to a work surface and knead for 10–15 minutes.

Once kneaded, add the TVP and knead again for 1 minute, or until just combined. Remove the seitan dough from the mixer and divide into 8 balls.

Gently roll the balls of dough into rough sausage shapes. Place each on an 8 x 6in (20 x 15cm) rectangle of parchment paper. Roll up tightly and twist the ends like a Christmas cracker. Wrap again tightly, this time in foil.

Set up a steamer. Steam the wrapped sausages for 1 hour, turning halfway through.

Allow them to cool to room temperature, then transfer to the fridge to chill for at least 1 hour before use.

To store, keep tightly wrapped and place in an airtight container in the fridge for up to 1 week, or in the freezer for up to 1 month.

Building Block Recipes:
Meats

Level ①②③

Seitan Chunks

Makes
3½lb (1.5kg)

Everyone needs a decent meaty chunk around the kitchen, ideal for all your cuboid plant-protein needs! But, you see, the best thing about these chunks is that they can actually be any shape you want! Shred them for a pulled pork vibe, slice them for beef strips, or stick with chunks for a beef bourguignon! The choice is yours and yours alone. Choose wisely. I'll be watching, silently, and judging.

For the poaching broth

5 quarts (5 liters) water
1 teaspoon black peppercorns
1 teaspoon mustard seeds
3 bay leaves
3 tablespoons dark soy sauce
2 teaspoons Marmite
3 tablespoons massel beef stock powder, or vegan mushroom bouillon powder
2 tablespoons light brown sugar
1 garlic bulb, sliced in half across the middle
4 thyme sprigs
4 rosemary sprigs
1 onion, quartered
1 carrot, quartered
2 celery ribs, quartered
Fine sea salt

For the seitan

10½oz (300g) pack silken tofu
14oz (400g) can cannellini beans, including the liquid
3 tablespoons dark soy sauce
2 teaspoons balsamic vinegar
2 tablespoons massel beef stock powder, or vegan mushroom bouillon powder
1 tablespoon liquid smoke
1 tablespoon red Bisto granules, or any other vegan gravy granules
1 teaspoon onion powder
¼ cup (60ml) flavorless vegetable oil, such as sunflower, rapeseed, or canola
3½ cups (400g) vital wheat gluten

To make the broth, fill a large saucepan for which you have a lid with the water and place over high heat. Bring to a boil. Add all the broth ingredients with 1 teaspoon salt, then reduce the heat to simmer and cover with a lid.

For the seitan, place everything except for the vital wheat gluten into the largest bowl of a high-speed blender and add 2 teaspoons salt. Blend on high speed for a minimum of 1 minute, pausing to scrape down the sides, then blend again until the mixture is completely smooth.

Add the vital wheat gluten and blend until smooth and very stretchy, 2–5 minutes. Stop the blender and rest for 10 minutes. Once rested, blend again for 1 minute more. The dough should be very stringy, almost the texture of chewing gum.

Remove the dough from the blender and knead lightly on a work surface until it comes together. Divide the dough into 8 pieces, roughly 5 ½oz (150g) each. Roll the portions of dough into balls, cover them with an upturned baking sheet and leave them to rest for 20 minutes.

Meanwhile, cut out 3 ½ x 9in (8 x 22cm) squares of muslin or cheesecloth. Set aside.

Working with 1 portion of dough at a time, roll the dough with the palms of your hands into a long snake, 12in (30cm) in length. Don't worry if the dough tries to spring back slightly.

Hold both ends of the length of dough and twist in opposite directions until the dough feels taut (5–6 full rotations). With the dough still twisted, tie in 2 knots and squeeze gently until the knots hold.

Place the knotted dough onto a square of muslin or cheesecloth. Tie opposing corners of the muslin or cheesecloth so the dough is tightly wrapped. Set aside and repeat with the remaining pieces of dough.

Building Block Recipes:
Meats

Level ① ② ③

Seitan Chunks

Equipment needed
High-speed blender

Once all the pieces of dough are knotted and wrapped, carefully place them in the simmering broth, cover with the lid, and reduce the temperature to the lowest setting.

Simmer the seitan for 1 hour. The seitan will float to the top and expand in size, so be sure to stir every 10 minutes or so. Do not allow the broth to come to a rolling boil; it should simmer very gently. If most of the broth evaporates, add more freshly boiled water.

Once cooked, turn off the heat and leave the pan of seitan and broth to cool to room temperature. Once at room temperature, unwrap the seitan and slice or tear into chunks.

Transfer the chunks to a container, cover with the broth, seal, and place in the fridge to chill and marinate for at least 4 hours or ideally overnight. The seitan is now ready to eat or broil, fry, roast, or cook however you like.

To store, keep the chunks sealed and submerged in the broth and refrigerate for up to 1 week, or freeze for up to 1 month.

Recipe note
In the photo, I've served the seitan chunks with rice noodles and veggies in a simple, spicy broth, but feel free to use however you would use chunks of beef or lamb.

Building Block Recipes:
Meats

Level ① ② ⟨3⟩

Seitan Deli Meat

Makes
2½lb (1.1kg)

For the poaching broth

5 quarts (5 liters) water

2 fresh raw beets, quartered

3 tablespoons massel beef stock powder, or vegan mushroom bouillon powder

3 tablespoons dark soy sauce

2 teaspoons Marmite

1 teaspoon black peppercorns

2 teaspoons yellow mustard seeds

1 teaspoon chili flakes

1 tablespoon cilantro seeds

1 teaspoon cloves

3 bay leaves

2 tablespoons light brown sugar

Fine sea salt

Sea salt flakes

For the seitan

10½oz (300g) pack silken tofu

7oz (200g) fresh raw beets, peeled and cubed

3 tablespoons vegetable oil

3 tablespoons English mustard

2 tablespoons massel beef stock powder, or vegan mushroom bouillon powder

1 tablespoon onion powder

2 tablespoons nutritional yeast

1 tablespoon rice vinegar, white wine vinegar, or apple cider vinegar

2 tablespoons liquid smoke

3 tablespoons dark soy sauce

3¾ cups (425g) vital wheat gluten

3½ tablespoons shredded vegetable suet

Equipment needed

High-speed blender (optional)

In school, my rather judgmental friends and I used to keep a mental log of everyone who had boring sandwiches for lunch. We had a theory that boring sandwiches equals boring person (peer-reviewed study pending). We even started to use "white-bread-one-filling" as an adjective to describe someone who was a bit of a snore-fest. I tend not to judge people by their food choices so much these days, but if you're interested in branching out in the sandwich department, this recipe is for you! Vegan deli meat, ideal for stacking in a massive sandwich that proves to the world you're a really interesting human and definitely not overcompensating.

To make the broth, fill a large saucepan for which you have a lid with the water and place over high heat. Bring to a boil. Add the beets, stock powder, dark soy sauce, and Marmite with 3 tablespoons fine sea salt, then reduce the heat to simmer and cover with a lid.

For the seitan, place all the ingredients except the vital wheat gluten and suet into a high-speed blender, add 2 teaspoons fine sea salt, and blend until very smooth. If your blender isn't high-speed, just get the mixture as smooth as possible. Place a sieve over a bowl and pour the mixture through.

Return the mixture to the blender and add the vital wheat gluten. Blend again until a smooth, very stretchy dough forms, almost the texture of chewing gum (around 5 minutes). If your blender struggles to manage the dough, remove half and blend the dough in 2 batches.

Turn off the blender and leave the dough to rest for 10 minutes. Once rested, add the suet and pulse-blend a few times, or until the flecks of suet are barely visible. Remove the dough from the blender, place on a work surface, and cover with an upturned bowl to prevent it from drying out.

Meanwhile, place the spices and bay leaves for the broth in a dry frying pan and place over low heat. Toast until fragrant, then transfer to a blender or spice grinder. Pulse-blend a few times until the spices are coarsely ground. Transfer to a bowl and mix in the sugar and 2 tablespoons sea salt flakes.

Add half the spice blend to the simmering broth, then sprinkle the rest over a work surface.

**Building Block Recipes:
Meats**

Level

Seitan Deli Meat

Uncover the seitan dough and roll with the palms of your hands into an 8in (20cm) cylinder. Roll the seitan dough in the spices to coat on all sides. Wrap the dough tightly in parchment paper, twisting the ends like a Christmas cracker. Wrap again in muslin or cheesecloth. Use chef's twine to tie up the seitan multiple times tightly along the length and around the circumference of the dough, like a joint of meat.

Carefully lower the wrapped seitan into the simmering broth and cover with a lid. Leave to simmer for 1½ hours, then turn off the heat and leave to cool to room temperature (ideally overnight). Once cooled, unwrap the seitan and slice thinly before serving.

To store, place in an airtight container in the fridge for up to 1 week, or in the freezer for up to 1 month.

> **Recipe note**
> In the photo here I've served the deli meat on a New York-style bagel with pickles, cream cheese, and mustard. Feel free to use yours however you'd use deli meat.

Paper Tofu Bacon

Makes 16

2 sheets paper tofu
¼ cup (60ml) dark soy sauce
2 tablespoons vegetable oil
3 tablespoons liquid smoke,
    or 1 tablespoon
    smoked paprika
1 tablespoon maple syrup
2 tablespoons beet juice
2 teaspoons rice flour,
    or cornstarch

Vegans will make bacon out of—and I say this with love—anything. Rice paper bacon, banana skin bacon, sandpaper bacon (only one of these is made up). The list is endless. My addition to that list is paper tofu bacon. I love it because it's high protein, it blisters and bubbles like real bacon, and it has the potential to be crispy or chewy, depending on how you like it. Find paper tofu in the fresh section of your local Asian supermarket. If you fancy making pepperoni from paper tofu as well, head to page 171.

Tear the paper tofu carefully into 16 bacon-size strips and place in a bowl.

In a separate small bowl, whisk together the remaining bacon ingredients to make a marinade. Pour over the tofu, coating each strip.

The bacon is ready to cook immediately, but if you have time, cover the bowl and leave in the fridge to marinate for 24 hours.

Preheat the broiler.

Remove the tofu strips from the marinade and arrange in ruffled waves on a baking sheet.

Place under the broiler on the top rack and broil for 2 minutes on each side (or 3 for crispy bacon), brushing with extra marinade when you flip the strips over. Serve immediately.

Building Block Recipes:
Meats

Level ① ② ③

Cheeses

Insisting you've never craved cheese is one of the Brownie badges of a gold-star vegan. Me, I'm a tin-star vegan, aluminum at best, because, BOY, did I miss cheese! Pretty quickly those cravings passed, but I still found myself with a big cheese-shaped hole in my life. What about my late-night snack of toast, Marmite, Cheddar, and sliced cucumbers (which I'm aware makes me sound a bit pregnant)? What about the genius move of topping yesterday's leftover pasta with mozzarella and broiling until golden and crisp? What about that time when the waiter sprinkled Parmesan on my pizza and asked me to "say when" and it turns out he's still sprinkling to this very day? These were all-important moments in my experience of being a human, and, fortunately, they don't need to end once you become vegan.

I've cracked a few codes, hacked a few mainframes, and jimmied a few padlocks to bring you four next-level vegan cheeses you can make from the comfort of your own home.

Are there ways to make vegan cheese from scratch at home?
Yep, absolutely! If you're looking for a long answer, there are loads of recipes out there for cultured vegan cheeses that follow traditional cheese-making processes, except using plant milks instead of dairy. But in this section I'm keeping things simple (because I had a whole book to write). I've whittled things down to four essentials: a melting mozzarella that browns under the broiler; a tangy, salty Parmesan for topping fancy pasta; a delicious sliceable Cheddar for stuffing in sandwiches; and a silky-smooth almond ricotta for spreading on toast. Use them wisely!

Building Block Recipes:
Cheeses

Vegan Mozzarella

Makes
23oz (650g)

10½oz (300g) silken tofu

3½oz (100ml) refined coconut oil, melted

½ teaspoon vegan lactic acid, or rice vinegar

3 tablespoons nutritional yeast

⅓ cup (60g) tapioca starch

2 tablespoons white miso paste

⅔ cup (160ml) water

Fine sea salt

Equipment needed

High-speed blender

This vegan cheese is a descendant of my most popular recipe of all time! Absolutely no pressure, mate... My original recipe was a superstar because it not only melted like mozzarella, but it also browned and went all crispy on the edges when broiled. This recipe, however, is better. It does everything I just mentioned but doesn't require you to soak cashews for six hours beforehand, meaning you can have fresh vegan mozzarella in a matter of minutes. That also means the recipe is completely free from nuts, gluten, and, obvs, dairy!

Place all the ingredients into the bowl of a high-speed blender with 1 teaspoon salt.

Blend until completely smooth (about 2 minutes), then transfer to a small saucepan.

Place the saucepan over medium-low heat. Whisking constantly, heat the mixture until it thickens very dramatically (about 5 minutes). Do not stop whisking until the mixture is thick and stringy, then remove from the heat.

The cheese is ready to use immediately: spoon over pizza or pasta and broil or bake until golden brown and bubbling. Alternatively, transfer to a fridge-safe storage container and cover loosely with a lid. Allow to cool to room temperature, then place in the fridge for up to 1 week (or the freezer for up to 1 month) and use as needed.

> **Recipe note**
> This cheese doesn't set firm like some other recipes. It's designed to be spooned or spread, then broiled or baked. It's ideal for all melting cheesy situations (think on top of shepherd's pie, French onion soup, and pizza) but I'd use my Sliceable Cheddar (see page 256) if you're after a sandwich filler.

Grateable Parmesan

Makes
1lb (450g)

7oz (200ml) soy milk
6 tablespoons refined
   coconut oil, melted
⅞ cup (140g) potato flour
1 tablespoon gram flour (aka
   chickpea or besan flour)
2 tablespoons white
   miso paste
4 tablespoons
   nutritional yeast
2 teaspoons vegan lactic
   acid powder, or sub for
   2 teaspoons rice vinegar
Fine sea salt
Sea salt flakes

Equipment needed
High-speed blender

Ninety-nine percent of vegan Parmesan recipes you'll encounter are made by blending cashews into a dust that you can sprinkle over pasta. That's cool, if you like eating dust. My Parmesan is a crumbly, craggy wedge like the real thing and is flecked with flaky salt crystals. It's got that bold, acidic tang you're after, too. You can grate it over spaghetti, add it to cheesy sauces, or even top your avocado toast with wafer-thin shreds. She's a versatile dairy-free queen and we love to see it!

Place a bamboo steamer over a pan of simmering water. Find a heatproof dish for which you have a lid (I use a rectangular Pyrex container) that will fit the steamer.

Place all the ingredients except the sea salt flakes in the bowl of a high-speed blender and add 2 teaspoons fine sea salt. Blend until smooth and glossy.

Add 1 teaspoon sea salt flakes and mix with a spoon until just combined.

Transfer the mixture to the heatproof dish. Cover loosely and place in a steamer to steam for 45 minutes, being sure to top off the water if necessary.

Remove from the steamer and take off the lid. Leave to cool on a work surface, uncovered, until at room temperature. Transfer to the fridge and leave to cool for at least 4 hours, or ideally overnight.

Once fully cooled, the mixture should have set firm. It's ready to use. Grate, shred, or slice and serve however you would a dairy Parmesan.

To store, place in an airtight container and keep in the fridge for up to 1 week, or the freezer for 1 month.

> **Recipe note**
> Potato flour is essential for that firm Parmesan crumble. I'd love to tell you that all starches work the same, but they don't, I've tried, so don't use cornstarch or tapioca flour instead. The vegan lactic acid, however, can be replaced by rice vinegar, if really necessary.

Sliceable Cheddar

Makes
1lb (450g)

7oz (200ml) soy milk

3oz (90ml) refined coconut oil, melted

1 cup (150g) potato flour

2 tablespoons white miso paste

2 tablespoons nutritional yeast

1 teaspoon onion powder

1 teaspoon English mustard

1 teaspoon tomato purée

1 teaspoon vegan lactic acid powder, or 2 teaspoons rice vinegar

Fine sea salt

Equipment needed

High-speed blender

When I was a kid, my dad enjoyed making us place a superthin slice of tangy Cheddar cheese on our tongues and leaving it there for as long as we could manage. I guess it was some sort of twisted lesson about delayed gratification, but now I'm an adult with defiance disorder, so it clearly didn't work. This recipe is my attempt to make a vegan version that's just as mouthwatering and irresistible, except I'll be disappointed if I see you using it for self-control training. I want to see you stuffing it in sandwiches, slicing it on cheese boards, and stacking it on crackers with pickles.

Place a bamboo steamer over a pan of simmering water. Find a heatproof dish for which you have a lid (I use a rectangular Pyrex container) that will fit the steamer.

Place all the ingredients in the cup of a high-speed blender with 1 teaspoon salt. Blend until smooth and glossy.

Transfer the blended mixture to the prepared dish in the steamer and cover loosely with the lid to stop any water from dripping in. Steam for 45 minutes, being sure to top off the water if necessary.

Remove from the steamer but do not remove the lid. Leave to cool on the work surface until the mixture reaches room temperature.

Transfer to the fridge and leave to set and chill for at least 4 hours, or ideally overnight.

Once fully chilled, the Cheddar should have set firm. It is ready to use. Grate, shred, or slice and serve however you would dairy Cheddar.

To store, place in an airtight container and keep in the fridge for up to 1 week or the freezer for 1 month.

Building Block Recipes:
Cheeses

Level ①〈2〉☼3☼

Almond Ricotta

Makes
7oz (200g)

⅔ cup (150g) flaked almonds
3¾ cups (750ml) water
3 tablespoons rice vinegar
Fine sea salt

Equipment needed
High-speed blender
Meat thermometer
 (optional)
Nut-milk bag

Plot-twist: not all vegan cheese needs nutritional yeast! Sure, I love to Scrooge McDuck swan-dive into a pool of nooch as much as the next guy, but save those nutty umami vibes for other recipes! Ricotta is more about texture than it is about cheesy flavor, so it was vital to me that this recipe hit that creamy mouthfeel sweet spot. This recipe uses homemade almond milk but mimics the process for a real dairy ricotta. The final product is *mwah: chef's kiss* and works equally well in sweet or savory dishes.

Place the almonds in the bowl of a high-speed blender along with the water and 3 teaspoons salt. Blend until you have a very smooth white milk.

Strain the almond milk through a fine nut-milk bag, discarding the almond pulp. Transfer the strained milk to a medium saucepan.

Place the milk over medium-low heat and gradually bring to 180°F (85°C), stirring constantly (if you don't have a cooking thermometer, heat the milk until steam begins to rise from the surface, but don't let it boil). At 180°F (85°C), add the vinegar and stir to combine. Cover the pan and leave the mixture to cool down to room temperature.

Place a clean nut-milk bag in a sieve and place over a bowl. Pour the liquid through. The bag will catch the almond milk curds. Gather the sides of the bag and very gently twist and squeeze the excess liquid through.

Suspend the nut-milk bag from the top shelf of your fridge with a container underneath to catch any drips. Leave to drain fully for a minimum of 6 hours, ideally overnight.

Using a teaspoon, pack the drained curds into a cheese mold or a ramekin (if you line this with muslin, as I did for this photo, it will give the appearance of a posh dairy ricotta). Return to the fridge for at least 24 hours to set before serving, and eat within 1 week.

Building Block Recipes:
Cheeses

Level

Quick Sauces

Loads of sauces aren't vegan, which is rubbish for lots of reasons. But it's also great because you get to make your own, from scratch. It also means you get to design your own sauce bottle label and stick it to a used jar, then feel great about your artistic talent every time you open the fridge. "Oh awesome, some delicious vegan barbecue sauce! And would you look at that label? It's transcendent! Did you buy this barbecue sauce in an art gallery?"

Remember that art teacher who laughed at your painting of a cow? Well, who's laughing now? You're a Turner Prize-nominated professional sauce-bottle designer who literally has no time to think about the past because you have so many sauce-bottle designs swimming around in your brain. And you're going to tell her that the next time you bump into her in the supermarket.

Wait, let me guess. Your God-tier sauces are *places fingers to temples* mayonnaise, ranch dressing, barbecue, and buffalo sauce? But of couuuurse they are, that was too easy! These pals are my drippy-dippy golden-boys! My french fry main gurls! They're the gosh-darn four horses of the apoco-dips here to herald the end of the line for gross, non-vegan condiments!

Those four, and the other sauces here, are fast to make and deliver a real punch without any animal products required. I keep jars full of them in my fridge at all times, which is a lie I just told, designed to convince you that I have my life in order. In truth, I don't, and my fridge is the dead giveaway. The only things I religiously keep in there are the ghosts of a thousand forgotten bagged salads.

Building Block Recipes:
Quick Sauces

Ten-Second Mayo

Makes
1⅔ cup (350g)

½ cup (120ml) soy milk
1 cup (240ml) sunflower oil
3 teaspoons rice vinegar
¼ teaspoon Dijon mustard
1 tablespoon cold-pressed
  rapeseed oil
Fine sea salt

Okay, maybe not ten seconds exactly, but like, really, really fast mayo. It works every time, but you will need to make sure your soy milk and sunflower oil are at room temperature before starting. Oh, and don't think you're special and decide to use extra-virgin olive oil because it's fancy. I see you, health-food vegans! Olive oil is too acidic and will cause the mayo to split, and then you'll have wasted a whole lot of olive oil.

Place all the ingredients in a tall container or small bowl with 1 teaspoon salt. Blend with an immersion blender until thick and creamy.

Transfer to a clean jar and store in the fridge for up to 1 week, or use immediately.

Building Block Recipes:
Quick Sauces

Level ①②③

Blender Ranch

Makes
1 cup (225g)

⅞ cup (200g) Ten-Second
   Mayo (see opposite), or
   store-bought vegan mayo
2 tablespoons soy milk
2 teaspoons garlic powder
2 teaspoons onion powder
2 tablespoons white
   wine vinegar
Small bunch parsley,
   stalks removed
Small bunch dill,
   stalks removed
2 tablespoons capers, drained
Fine sea salt and freshly
   ground black pepper

I first tried ranch as a sheltered teenager visiting America. I loved it so much that I tried to smuggle a bottle back home with me in my suitcase. Things didn't work out, and I lost my entire collection of ironic wolf T-shirts to the largest ranch-based pressurized cabin accident of 2005. Later, as I dunked a panic batch of oven chips into my open suitcase, I realized, "Yeah, I really could've just made this stuff from scratch." So I did.

Place all the ingredients in a food processor with ½ teaspoon salt and ¼ teaspoon pepper and blend until smooth.

Transfer to a clean jar and store in the fridge for up to 1 week, or use immediately.

Building Block Recipes:
Quick Sauces

Level ① ② ③

Buffalo Sauce

Makes
¾ cup (180g)

½ cup (113g) Vegan Butter
(see page 272), or store-
bought vegan butter
¼ cup (60ml) hot sauce
2 tablespoons white
wine vinegar
1 teaspoon soy sauce
¼ teaspoon garlic powder

Hot 'n' glossy! Two adjectives that describe both this sauce and my brow after eating it. The best hot sauce for buffalo is hotly disputed, with most recipes settling on Frank's RedHot, but some diehards insist on Crystal. I've tried this recipe with just about every vegan hot sauce I can get my hands on, and I remain loyal to Valentina, but you do you! Just avoid anything CRAZY spicy, since we're already using a decent quantity in this recipe.

Place all the ingredients in a small saucepan and bring to a simmer.

Whisking constantly, simmer until the butter is completely melted, then remove from the heat. Serve hot.

Gochujang Barbecue Sauce

Makes
¾ cup (150g)

3 tablespoons gochujang
2 tablespoons dark
soy sauce
2 tablespoons liquid smoke
5 tablespoons ketchup
1 teaspoon garlic powder
2 tablespoons maple syrup,
or agave syrup

IMHO, barbecue sauce should be smoky, hot, and a bit funky. So, naturally I chuck a load of gochujang in there. I love the fermented umami kick it brings, and the spice is mellow, not numbing. Now your only challenge is not putting this sauce on everything.

Place all the ingredients in a small saucepan and bring to a simmer.

Simmer for 4–5 minutes, then remove from the heat and allow to cool.

Transfer to a clean jar and store in the fridge for up to 3 weeks, or use right away.

Building Block Recipes:
Quick Sauces

Level

Zankou Garlic Whip

Makes
1¾ cup (400g)

20 garlic cloves, peeled
Juice of 1 lemon
1½ cups (350ml) vegetable
oil, at room temperature
3 tablespoons ice-cold water
Sea salt flakes

It's not often that people take restaurant recommendations from a true-crime podcast, but when I heard about Zankou chicken via *My Favorite Murder*, I just knew I had to make a pilgrimage. It's a tiny LA-based family chain that grew out of Little Armenia and gained a cult interest following the murders committed by its owner (I'll leave a brief break here for you to have a Google).

However, it wasn't morbid fascination that drew me in—it was their infamous garlic sauce. They serve lots of it with everything, and, yet, I'd still recommend you order extra. It's silky smooth, impossibly creamy, and bright white, with a punch of raw garlic balanced by a gentle acidity. The recipe is top secret, but I've done my best to make a replica from taste. It's not the real thing, but it's kept me sane between trips to LA.

Place the garlic cloves in a food processor with the lemon juice and 1 teaspoon salt.

Pulse-blend in the food processor until a paste forms, then run on high speed until the paste is completely smooth.

With the processor running, add one-third of the oil in a very slow drizzle, followed by 1 tablespoon of the water. Repeat the process until all the oil and all the water have been added. The mixture should be light, fluffy, and bright white.

Stored in the fridge in an airtight container, this should keep for up to 1 week.

Building Block Recipes:
Quick Sauces

Level ①〈2〉⟨3⟩

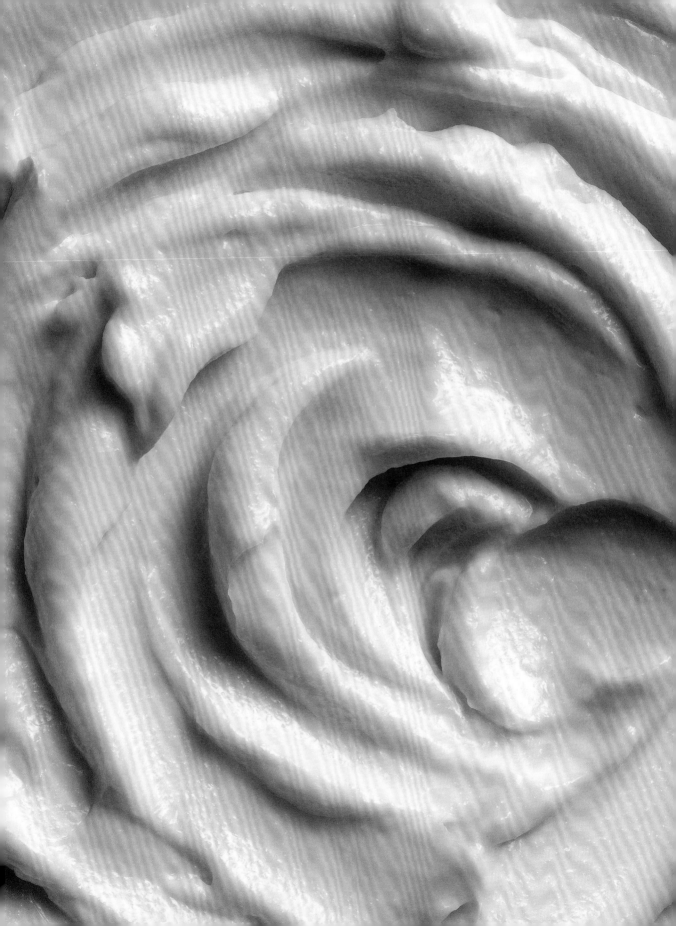

"If It Ain't Yolk" Sauce

Makes
¾ cup (200g)

1¾ cups (200g) grated
   carrot, or ¼ cup (60ml)
   carrot juice
½ teaspoon white wine
   vinegar
¼ teaspoon kala namak
   (black salt)
5 tablespoons Vegan Butter
   (see page 272), or
   store-bought vegan
   butter, melted
¼ cup (60g) cold-pressed
   rapeseed oil

With this recipe, I set myself the challenge of creating a sauce that could replace runny egg yolk in all your plant-based breakfasts… and I nailed it *the crowd goes wiiiiiiiiiiiiiiiild*. But wait, there's more *the crowd falls hushed and intrigued*. This sauce has since taken over my kitchen and can be found on everything from rice bowls to sandwiches; I genuinely can't eat a meal without it! And guess what? It takes minutes to make and involves zero cooking! *the crowd bursts into a chant: "IT AIN'T YOLK! IT AIN'T YOLK! IT AIN'T YOLK!"*

Place the grated carrot, if using, in a nut-milk bag or on a piece of muslin or cheesecloth and wring all the juice out into a bowl. You'll need ¼ cup (60ml) of carrot juice, so measure and keep wringing until you reach the right amount. Keep the drained carrot shreds for use in carrot cake or smoothies.

Place the carrot juice in a food processor along with the vinegar and kala namak. Blend until combined.

In a separate measuring cup, whisk together the melted vegan butter and rapeseed oil. With the food processor running, pour in the vegan butter and oil in a slow steady stream until combined and smooth.

Transfer the yolk sauce to a jar or squeezy sauce bottle and allow to cool to room temperature before serving. To store, keep sealed in the fridge for up to 2 weeks. Microwave for 10 seconds and shake well before use.

> **Recipe note**
> Vegetable oil works well here, too, but it doesn't have the bright golden gloss of cold-pressed rapeseed oil. The rapeseed oil is largely responsible for the color of the sauce, so if you're going for yolky, stick to rapeseed oil.

Building Block Recipes:
Quick Sauces

Level ① ② ③

Makin Marinara

2 tablespoons olive oil
1 red onion, chopped
5 garlic cloves, halved
½ teaspoon chili flakes
7oz (200ml) vegan red wine
1 teaspoon sugar
3 tablespoons tomato purée
1 tablespoon dried oregano
Leaves of 2 basil sprigs, torn
2 x 14oz (400g) cans plum
    tomatoes
⅔ cup (160ml) water
Fine sea salt and freshly
    ground black pepper

Everyone thinks they know best when it comes to their marinara sauce. That's okay. All I know is that I cook this recipe about six times an hour and have never once regretted putting five cloves of garlic in anything. I use it in a few recipes throughout the book, so my advice is to prep some in advance and jar it up. Go on, live out your cottage-core fantasy!

Place a medium saucepan for which you have a lid over medium heat and pour in the olive oil. Once hot, add the onion, garlic, and chili flakes. Fry until the onion is soft, then add the red wine and sugar.

Simmer until the wine has reduced in volume by half, about 3 minutes.

Stir in the tomato purée, dried oregano, basil, 1 teaspoon salt, and ¼ teaspoon pepper. Cook for 1 minute or until bubbling hot.

Add the tomatoes and water. Bring to a simmer, then reduce the heat to medium-low and cover with the lid. Simmer for at least 20 minutes (ideally 40), stirring occasionally.

Remove the lid and use a potato masher to crush the tomatoes and garlic until you have a chunky sauce. Serve immediately, or refrigerate for 3–4 days, or freeze, or transfer to a sterilized jar (see above right) and store in a cool place for up to 1 year.

> **Recipe note**
> If you do plan to jar up this sauce, be sure to sterilize some jars to make sure everything stays safe to eat! The easiest way is to wash your jars and lids in warm soapy water, then rinse them, but do not dry them. Place upside down on a baking sheet lined with parchment paper and place in an oven preheated to 325°F (175°C) convection for 15 minutes. Once cooled, they're ready.

Vegan Butter

**Makes
1½ cups (350g)**

½ cup (120ml) soy milk
⅞ cup (180g) refined
    coconut oil, melted
1 teaspoon lemon juice
2 tablespoons white
    miso paste
1 teaspoon sunflower
    lecithin
Sea salt flakes

Equipment needed
High-speed blender

Yes! You can make your own vegan butter that is salty and creamy and perfect on everything from crusty baguettes to freshly baked scones! My personal fave activity is spreading some on an English muffin, followed by a near-fatal dredge of Marmite and watching the glossy emulsion melt right through like a fancy, rain showerhead. Speaking of showers, sounds like I need a cold one. #hotforcrumpets

Blend all the ingredients together with ½ teaspoon salt in a high-speed blender until thick and smooth.

Pour into a butter mold or empty margarine tub, cover, then refrigerate for 8 hours.

To store, transfer the butter to an airtight container and refrigerate for up to 1 week.

> **Recipe note**
> You may be unfamiliar with liquid lecithin, but I strongly recommend adding it to your list of vegan pantry staples. Lecithin is an emulsifier that occurs naturally in egg yolks, soybeans, and sunflower seeds. In this recipe, it's essential for holding the fats and liquids together in an emulsion, leaving you with a silky-smooth vegan butter.

Building Block Recipes:
Quick Sauces

Level ①②③

Suppliers

Condensed and Evaporated Coconut Milk
- Instacart.com
- Whole Foods: Wholefoodsmarket.com (in-store and online)
- Wegman's: Wegmans.com (in-store and online)
- Shoprite
- Kroger
- Aldi
- Walmart: Walmart.com (in-store and online)

Refined Coconut Oil
- Instacart: Instacart.com
- Freshdirect.com
- Vitacost.com
- Thrivemarket.com
- Target: Target.com (in-store and online)

Kala Namak
- Indian specialty supermarkets
- iherb.com
- Ranibrand.com
- Vitacost.com
- Thrivemarket.com
- Savorypantry.com

Kombu
- Asian specialty supermarkets
- Whole Foods: Wholefoodsmarket.com (in-store and online)
- Thrivemarket.com
- Hivebrands.com

Liquid Lecithin
- Health Food Stores
- Vitaminshoppe.com
- Instacart.com
- iherb.com
- Walmart

Massel Stock
- Amazon.com
- Walmart.com
- Fodyfoods.com

Paper Tofu
- Asian specialty supermarkets
- Freshdirect.com
- Sayweee.com

Psyllium Husk Powder
- Asian specialty supermarkets
- Health food stores
- Whole Foods: Wholefoodsmarket.com (In-store and online)
- Vitaminshoppe.com
- Walmart: Walmart.com (in-store and online)

Tapioca Starch
- Instacart.com
- Thrivemarket.com
- Freshdirect.com
- Healthyfoods.com
- Whole Foods: Wholefoodsmarket.com (In-store and online)

Vegan Lactic Acid
- Whole Foods
- Amazon.com
- Mezzonifoods.com

Vital Wheat Gluten
- Asian specialty supermarkets
- Nuts.com
- Kingarthurbaking.com
- Freshdirect.com
- Walmart

Yuba
- Asian specialty supermarkets
- Umani-insider.store
- Freshdirect.com
- Amazon.com

Index

Thank you

This is probably the only point in this book where I'll be deliberately earnest, so don't get used to it. I cannot explain how long I've dreamed of writing a cookbook, and even though it's very real now, it still hasn't sunk in properly. Without these people below, this book you're holding simply wouldn't exist, so with sincerity, thank you:

Bloomsbury
When I found out I'd be working with Bloomsbury on my first book, my knees literally buckled. Thank you for believing in me and this project.

Rowan Yapp
Thank you for your cool and ever-rational approach to a really complicated project. You've helped me navigate one of the biggest challenges I've ever faced: writing a cookbook during a pandemic. And you've given me so much freedom to create something special right from square one.

Richard Pike
You engaged with my vision from the point when this book was just a two-page proposal and you backed it with more gusto than I thought possible. Thanks for taking a chance on this one.

Kitty Stogdon
For everything you've done to hold this project together and for always laughing visibly at my poorly timed jokes during Zoom meetings.

Lucy Bannell
For your patience, meticulous eye for detail, and investment in this book. You nurtured my voice throughout and tolerated dozens more dad jokes than contractually obliged.

Ella and Guy
As I type this, you're driving four hours to Hastings to help me take some selfies for the book. You've made my words and photos look more beautiful than I could've ever imagined. You encouraged me to be bold and it really paid off. I'm so lucky to have your support.

Lillie
I'm so glad Instagram recognized our compatible brands of chaotic-good energy and brought us together. You reminded me that cooking is supposed to be a laugh when all I wanted to do was scream into a pillow.

Mike and Claire at Good on Greens
I knew vegetables were going to be important for this project, but
I couldn't have known how key our friendship would be. Thank you for
your warmth and for being the best greengrocers I've ever known.

**Alice Levine, Lauren Toyota, Timothy Pakron, Derek Sarno,
Liz Nguyĕn, and Joe Tam**
The inspiration and advice you've given me throughout this process
has been so generous. Thank you for your expert guidance; I truly
owe you one.

Ripley
I know you can't read this because you're a dog, but I hope you know
how important you are to me. Every time you trotted down to the
basement kitchen because you heard me open a jar of peanut butter,
you brought me back to earth and kept me focused on what matters:
unconditional love and endless compassion.

Mam and Deedee
For teaching me to lead with love and always making me eat my
greens. You taught me that nothing affects change like sharing your
passion. You both inspire me every single day. ALYSM.

Bean and Teems
For the love, supportive energy, and occasional writing material.
Thank you for being part of this story.

Squange
On our first date, when I spoke about my future plans and your eyes lit
up, I knew you had my back. You've believed in me ever since and lifted
me up every step of this journey. I think you're the bee's knees.

Nanny Dartboard
I hope I grow up to be as brave as you. I always leave our chats feeling
happier and more motivated. Your courage, strength, and sense of
humor are more inspirational than you'll ever know.

Richard Makin

Richard Makin is the School Night Vegan. Richard has been exploring the world of plant-based cuisine since November 2017, when he switched from lifelong vegetarian to full-time vegan. Back then, he worked in street food, running London's first artisan ice-cream-sandwich van, so his weekends were usually way too busy for cooking. This meant that all his school nights became vegan nights!

As a long-time food obsessive, he had developed some pretty good cooking skills, but turning vegan was a whole new challenge. He had to retrain himself to cook without animal products—a surprisingly rewarding learning curve! He is now a food stylist, recipe developer, and food editor specializing in animal-free dishes.

schoolnightvegan.com schoolnightvegan @schoolnightvegan

About the Author

an imprint of Insight Editions
P.O. Box 3088
San Rafael, CA 94912
www.insighteditions.com

CEO Raoul Goff
VP Publisher Roger Shaw
Editorial Director Katie Killebrew
Editorial Assistant Kayla Belser
VP Creative Chrissy Kwasnik
Art Director Allister Fein
VP Manufacturing Alix Nicholaeff
Production Manager Joshua Smith
Sr Production Manager, Subsidiary
    Rights Lina s Palma-Temena

New Seed Press would also like to
thank Margaret Parrish.

First published in Great Britain in
2023 by Bloomsbury Publishing Plc.

Text © 2023 Richard Makin
Photography © 2023 Richard Makin

ISBN: 979-8-88674-059-2

Manufactured in China
10 9 8 7 6 5 4 3 2 1